Vegetarian Diets

ISSUES

Volume 214

Series Editor
Lisa Firth

Independence
Educational Publishers
Cambridge

First published by Independence
The Studio, High Green
Great Shelford
Cambridge CB22 5EG
England

British Library Cataloguing in Publication Data

Vegetarian diets. -- (Issues ; v. 214)
1. Vegetarianism. 2. Veganism. 3. Animal welfare--Moral and ethical aspects.
I. Series II. Firth, Lisa.
179.3-dc23

ISBN-13: 978 1 86168 594 0

Printed in Great Britain

MWL Print Group Ltd

CONTENTS

Chapter 1 Going Meat Free

Chapter 2 Vegetarianism and the Environment

Chapter 3 Vegetarian Nutrition

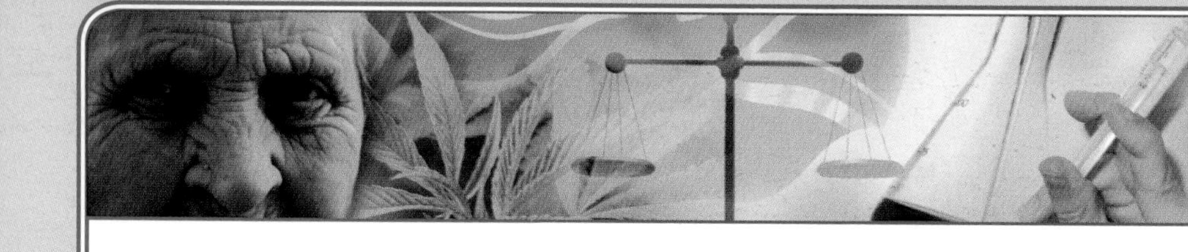

OTHER TITLES IN THE ISSUES SERIES

For more on these titles, visit: www.independence.co.uk

Sustainability and Environment ISBN 978 1 86168 419 6
A Classless Society? ISBN 978 1 86168 422 6
Migration and Population ISBN 978 1 86168 423 3
Sexual Orientation and Society ISBN 978 1 86168 440 0
The Gender Gap ISBN 978 1 86168 441 7
Domestic Abuse ISBN 978 1 86168 442 4
Travel and Tourism ISBN 978 1 86168 443 1
The Problem of Globalisation ISBN 978 1 86168 444 8
The Internet Revolution ISBN 978 1 86168 451 6
An Ageing Population ISBN 978 1 86168 452 3
Poverty and Exclusion ISBN 978 1 86168 453 0
Waste Issues ISBN 978 1 86168 454 7
Staying Fit ISBN 978 1 86168 455 4
Drugs in the UK ISBN 978 1 86168 456 1
The AIDS Crisis ISBN 978 1 86168 468 4
Bullying Issues ISBN 978 1 86168 469 1
Marriage and Cohabitation ISBN 978 1 86168 470 7
Our Human Rights ISBN 978 1 86168 471 4
Privacy and Surveillance ISBN 978 1 86168 472 1
The Animal Rights Debate ISBN 978 1 86168 473 8
Body Image and Self-Esteem ISBN 978 1 86168 484 4
Abortion – Rights and Ethics ISBN 978 1 86168 485 1
Racial and Ethnic Discrimination ISBN 978 1 86168 486 8
Sexual Health ISBN 978 1 86168 487 5
Selling Sex ISBN 978 1 86168 488 2
Citizenship and Participation ISBN 978 1 86168 489 9
Health Issues for Young People ISBN 978 1 86168 500 1
Crime in the UK ISBN 978 1 86168 501 8
Reproductive Ethics ISBN 978 1 86168 502 5
Tackling Child Abuse ISBN 978 1 86168 503 2
Money and Finances ISBN 978 1 86168 504 9
The Housing Issue ISBN 978 1 86168 505 6
Teenage Conceptions ISBN 978 1 86168 523 0
Work and Employment ISBN 978 1 86168 524 7
Understanding Eating Disorders ISBN 978 1 86168 525 4
Student Matters ISBN 978 1 86168 526 1
Cannabis Use ISBN 978 1 86168 527 8
Health and the State ISBN 978 1 86168 528 5
Tobacco and Health ISBN 978 1 86168 539 1
The Homeless Population ISBN 978 1 86168 540 7
Coping with Depression ISBN 978 1 86168 541 4
The Changing Family ISBN 978 1 86168 542 1
Bereavement and Grief ISBN 978 1 86168 543 8
Endangered Species ISBN 978 1 86168 544 5
Responsible Drinking ISBN 978 1 86168 555 1
Alternative Medicine ISBN 978 1 86168 560 5
Censorship Issues ISBN 978 1 86168 558 2
Living with Disability ISBN 978 1 86168 557 5
Sport and Society ISBN 978 1 86168 559 9
Self-Harming and Suicide ISBN 978 1 86168 556 8
Sustainable Transport ISBN 978 1 86168 572 8
Mental Wellbeing ISBN 978 1 86168 573 5
Child Exploitation ISBN 978 1 86168 574 2
The Gambling Problem ISBN 978 1 86168 575 9
The Energy Crisis ISBN 978 1 86168 576 6
Nutrition and Diet ISBN 978 1 86168 577 3
Coping with Stress ISBN 978 1 86168 582 7
Consumerism and Ethics ISBN 978 1 86168 583 4
Genetic Modification ISBN 978 1 86168 584 1
Education and Society ISBN 978 1 86168 585 8
The Media ISBN 978 1 86168 586 5
Biotechnology and Cloning ISBN 978 1 86168 587 2
International Terrorism ISBN 978 1 86168 592 6
The Armed Forces ISBN 978 1 86168 593 3
Vegetarian Diets ISBN 978 1 86168 594 0
Religion in Society ISBN 978 1 86168 595 7
Tackling Climate Change ISBN 978 1 86168 596 4
Euthanasia and Assisted Suicide ISBN 978 1 86168 597 1

A note on critical evaluation

Because the information reprinted here is from a number of different sources, readers should bear in mind the origin of the text and whether the source is likely to have a particular bias when presenting information (just as they would if undertaking their own research). It is hoped that, as you read about the many aspects of the issues explored in this book, you will critically evaluate the information presented. It is important that you decide whether you are being presented with facts or opinions. Does the writer give a biased or an unbiased report? If an opinion is being expressed, do you agree with the writer?

Vegetarian Diets offers a useful starting point for those who need convenient access to information about the many issues involved. However, it is only a starting point. Following each article is a URL to the relevant organisation's website, which you may wish to visit for further information.

Chapter 1

GOING MEAT FREE

What is a vegetarian?

Information from Veggie Advisor.

Vegetarians often encounter confusion about their diet, with many unsure about what a vegetarian can and cannot eat. If I tell someone I am vegetarian, the conversation usually proceeds with 'do you eat fish?' followed by 'do you eat dairy products?'. Some of this stems from people with different kinds of diets labelling themselves as vegetarian.

To clarify things, here are the definitions of the different kind of meat-free diets:

Vegetarian

Someone who does not eat meat, fish, poultry or any slaughterhouse by-product such as gelatine. (Provided by the Vegetarian Society.)

Vegan

Someone who does not eat meat, fish, poultry, dairy products, eggs, honey or any other animal product.

Pescetarian

Occasionally used to describe those who abstain from eating all meat and animal flesh with the exception of fish (this diet is not vegetarian).

Do you eat fish?

The pescetarian diet is not a vegetarian diet: however, many pescetarians will label themselves as vegetarians, much to the annoyance of many 'real' vegetarians. As a vegetarian myself, this can be a little frustrating, but I can understand why it happens, since 'pescetarian' is not a widely used or understood term. When dining away from home, pescetarians probably find it's easier to say they are 'vegetarian' to avoid being fed meat. Many vegetarians question the motives of pescetarians, and criticise them for consuming fish whilst abstaining from other animals. However, I have a positive attitude to those who eat only fish, since to me, any change towards the consumption of less meat can only be a positive one, whatever a person's reasons or motivations. Even a vegetarian diet is a compromise in many ways, since the dairy industry is not without cruelty and suffering. I therefore have a lot of admiration for vegans, even though I am not one myself. In the same regard, I also respect those meat eaters who make an effort to reduce their meat consumption. To me any reduction in meat intake is better than none at all! This leads to the recently coined term 'flexitarian'.

Flexitarian

Someone who eats a mostly vegetarian diet, with occasional meat consumption.

This term is good for describing the 'nearly' or 'part-time' vegetarians. I would guess that many true vegetarians probably started out this way on the path to vegetarianism, as opposed to suddenly cutting out meat altogether. My parents first started to reduce the family meat intake when I was four years old, and it wasn't until I was eight that we had cut out meat and fish entirely. As I mentioned before, I think that any reduction in meat intake can only be a positive step, so I don't have a problem with this kind of diet becoming more popular. The level of abstention from meat and animal products has always been a continuum, with people falling along different points of the scale. Having clear terms to describe the different points on the scale can only be a good thing!

⇨ The above information is reprinted with kind permission from Veggie Advisor. Visit www.veggieadvisor.com for more information.

VEGGIE ADVISOR

Understanding different types of vegetarianism

Confused about different veggie diets? Paula Carnogoy has the answers.

By Paula Carnogoy

What is a vegetarian? On the surface, that sounds like an easy question. A vegetarian is someone who doesn't eat meat. But where exactly do you draw the line? Is fish or other seafood considered to be meat? What about eggs and dairy products? These and similar questions can lead to some confusion over what exactly constitutes a vegetarian diet.

Broadly speaking, the following are the most common terms applied to vegetarians:

Vegetarians

Most people who describe themselves simply as vegetarian will refuse to eat any kind of animal flesh, including red and white meat, fish and seafood, and products derived from the bodies of animals such as gelatin. As a rule of thumb, if an animal had to die in order for the item to be produced, it is off the menu for vegetarians. On that basis, eggs and dairy products are acceptable.

Semi-vegetarians

This term is sometimes used for people who don't swear off eating meat altogether, but they do avoid certain types of animal products. For example, they might only eat white meat like poultry, seafood or fish, while avoiding beef, pork and other red meats. Or a semi-vegetarian might restrict their meat consumption to rare occasions.

Some 'real' vegetarians are scornful of the term semi-vegetarian, on the basis that you are either vegetarian or you are not. Others will argue that any attempt to reduce meat consumption should be applauded, and will encourage a semi-vegetarian diet among those who aren't ready to go the whole way.

Ovo-lacto vegetarians

Ovo-lacto vegetarians are people who don't eat any kind of meat or fish, but who do consume eggs and dairy products, including cheese, butter and milk. Some vegetarians restrict themselves to only one part of this category: ovo-vegetarians eat eggs but no dairy products, whereas lacto-vegetarians eat dairy but not eggs.

Vegans

Vegans don't eat any animal products whatsoever. Even such items as honey, which is produced by bees, are off the table. Vegans are sometimes called 'strict vegetarians', but that term is somewhat misleading as it can also be applied to any vegetarian who is particularly conscientious in keeping to their chosen diet.

Raw-food diet

Some vegetarians will take their dietary principles a step farther and eat only raw foods. The idea is that many of the important vitamins and nutrients in food are destroyed in the cooking process. People following a raw-food diet (sometimes called a living-food diet) believe that eating uncooked fruits, vegetables, nuts and seeds is healthier and better for the environment.

Fruitarians

Fruitarians eat only raw fruit and seeds. Unlike followers of a raw-food diet, they don't even eat vegetables, in the belief that the cultivation of vegetables contributes to the destruction of the environment through agriculture.

⇨ The above information is reprinted with kind permission from Veg World. Visit their website at www.veg-world.com for more information on this and other related topics.

A lacto-ovo vegetarian meets a fruitarian.

VEG WORLD

Veganism in a nutshell

Information from The Vegetarian Resource Group.

What is a vegan?

Vegetarians do not eat meat, fish or poultry. Vegans, in addition to being vegetarian, do not use other animal products and by-products such as eggs, dairy products, honey, leather, fur, silk, wool, cosmetics, and soaps derived from animal products.

Why veganism?

People choose to be vegan for health, environmental and/or ethical reasons. For example, some vegans feel that one promotes the meat industry by consuming eggs and dairy products. That is, once dairy cows or egg-laying chickens are too old to be productive, they are often sold as meat; and since male calves do not produce milk, they usually are raised for veal or other products. Some people avoid these items because of conditions associated with their production.

Many vegans choose this lifestyle to promote a more humane and caring world. They know they are not perfect, but believe they have a responsibility to try to do their best, while not being judgmental of others.

Vegan nutrition

The key to a nutritionally sound vegan diet is variety. A healthy and varied vegan diet includes fruits, vegetables, plenty of leafy greens, whole-grain products, nuts, seeds and legumes.

Protein

It is very easy for a vegan diet to meet the recommendations for protein as long as calorie intake is adequate. Strict protein planning or combining is not necessary. The key is to eat a varied diet.

Almost all foods except for alcohol, sugar and fats provide some protein. Vegan sources include: lentils, chickpeas, tofu, peas, peanut butter, soy milk, almonds, spinach, rice, whole-wheat bread, potatoes, broccoli, kale...

For example, if part of a day's menu included the following foods, you would meet the Recommended Dietary Allowance (RDA) for protein for an adult male:

- 1 cup oatmeal, 1 cup soy milk
- 2 slices whole-wheat bread, 1 bagel
- 2 tablespoons peanut butter
- 1 cup vegetarian baked beans
- 5 ounces tofu, 2 tablespoons of almonds
- 1 cup broccoli and 1 cup brown rice.

Common vegan foods

Oatmeal, stir-fried vegetables, cereal, toast, orange juice, peanut butter on whole-wheat bread, frozen fruit desserts, lentil soup, salad bar items like chickpeas and three-bean salad, dates, apples, macaroni, fruit smoothies, popcorn, spaghetti, vegetarian baked beans, guacamole, chili...

Vegans also eat...

Tofu lasagna, homemade pancakes without eggs, houmous, eggless cookies, soy ice cream, tempeh, corn chowder, soy yogurt, rice pudding, fava beans, banana muffins, spinach pies, oat nut burgers, falafel, corn fritters, French toast made with soy milk, soy hot dogs, vegetable burgers, pumpkin casserole, scrambled tofu, seitan.

When eating out try these foods

Pizza without cheese, Chinese moo shu vegetables, Indian curries and dahl, eggplant dishes without the cheese, bean tacos without the lard and cheese (available from Mexican restaurants), Middle Eastern houmous and tabouli, Ethiopian injera (flat bread) and lentil stew, Thai vegetable curries...

➪ The above information is reprinted with kind permission from The Vegetarian Resource Group. Visit www.vrg.org for more information.

THE VEGETARIAN RESOURCE GROUP

Vegetarianism: a brief history

Information from Henderson's of Edinburgh.

It is not so many years ago in this country that vegetarians were widely considered to be 'cranks' – the name chosen, with self-deprecating humour, by the establishment that opened its doors in Carnaby Street at the start of the sixties, beating Henderson's by a few months to the title of the UK's first vegetarian restaurant. Well, a glance at famous vegetarians through history throws up such names as Pythagoras and Plato, Confucius, Kafka, Tolstoy, Einstein, Wagner, Gandhi and Leonardo da Vinci. If vegetarians are cranks, it would seem, they are cranks in pretty good company.

The first usage of the term 'vegetarian' noted in the Oxford English Dictionary was as recently as 1839 – the practice and philosophy of vegetarianism, however, is far older than that. Indeed, some people have argued that mankind's diet originally consisted of berries, fruits, vegetables, seeds and nuts, and that early man only turned to meat-eating after climate change – another term with strikingly contemporary connotations – brought about massive changes to his habitat. Other scholars, it must be confessed, would dispute this point; what is certain, though, is that written sources show that vegetarianism was established and accepted by many of the peoples of ancient India at least as early as the ninth century BC. Of the major religions of India, Jainism has always advocated strict vegetarianism, while we find a slightly more compromised form in early Vedic, Hindu and Buddhist writings. Even today it is estimated that over 70% of the world's vegetarians live in India.

The first usage of the term 'vegetarian' noted in the Oxford English Dictionary was as recently as 1839

All this was to change during the age of Romanticism and Radicalism that followed the revolution in France, and by the first quarter of the 19th century vegetarianism had acquired such champions as the poet Shelley, author of *A Vindication of Natural Diet* and a passionate and vehement advocate of abstinence from meat (as well as atheism, free love and anything else that took his fancy). The movement gathered momentum as the century wore on, and the Vegetarian Society, the world's first, was formed in Ramsgate in 1847. It was soon followed by other societies throughout Europe, particularly Northern Europe, and the United States, where the American Vegetarian Society was founded in 1850. These national societies were amalgamated under the *aegis* of the International Vegetarian Union in 1908.

Throughout the 20th century, vegetarianism remained a respected but minority lifestyle; that changed again in the atmosphere of the 1960s which, perhaps because of a growing interest in Eastern religion and philosophy, saw an unprecedented upsurge in vegetarianism which since then has just grown and grown. It is difficult to imagine today a situation that was once painfully common, in which a vegetarian scans the menu in a restaurant and finds absolutely nothing they can eat.

The reasons why people choose to become vegetarians are probably as numerous as vegetarians themselves, but they could generally be grouped under three headings: ethics, health and the environment.

Many people turn to vegetarianism because they have been sickened by some of the practices of intensive farming, the battery farming of chickens being a prime example. While for some organic and free range meat production provide an answer to their moral dilemmas, for others all exploitation of animals, no matter how well they are treated during their lifetimes, is quite simply wrong. This is the modern equivalent of the 'abstinence from beings with a soul' philosophy of the ancient Greeks.

The principle underlying the practice of vegetarianism in ancient India was subtly different, though no less pertinent to vegetarians today. The guiding principle here was known as 'ahisma', roughly translated as the avoidance of doing harm, or non-violence. It is the principle that lies behind much Hindu and Buddhist thought in many fields, not just diet. The 'satyagraha', or non-violent civil disobedience of Gandhi, for example, was firmly rooted in this principle, which aims ultimately at nothing less than breaking forever the world's cycle of violence and destruction.

With regards to vegetarianism and health, once again attitudes have been transformed from the days when it was widely held that 'it's your meat that makes you bonnie'! It is now known not only that a vegetarian diet is viable and capable of providing all the body's nutritional needs, but that it does so with lower levels of saturated fats and cholesterol and significantly higher levels of fibre and antioxidants. Studies have shown that vegetarians tend to have lower body mass index, lower blood pressure and less incidence of heart disease, type 2 diabetes, osteoporosis and certain forms of dementia and cancer. The better general health and greater longevity of southern relative to northern Europe has long been noted, even within a single country, such as Italy when we compare the population south of the Alps, brought up on olive oil and fresh fruit and vegetables, with those of the north who are reliant more on butter and other animal-based fats. That being the case in Italy, it is surely not difficult to see the health benefits a vegetarian diet might bring in Scotland – a country in

HENDERSON'S OF EDINBURGH

which, as F. Marian McNeill, the doyenne of Scottish cookery writers, once noted, the general population do not eat vegetables unless they are in soup.

Another reason for the upsurge in vegetarianism in the past few decades has been the rise in environmental concerns which have accompanied it. There are of course lies, damned lies and statistics: nonetheless, reputable studies in recent years have suggested, among other things, that emissions from meat production account for 18% of the world's greenhouse gases; and that the same volume of crops could support ten times the number of people on a vegetarian diet than meat eaters. When a UN report concludes that the livestock sector is one of the top three contributors to the most serious environmental problems we face, little wonder many people are reassessing their dietary habits.

Before we get too serious about all this though, it is worth thinking about one other reason why so many people are now taking to vegetarianism: because the food is so delicious. Towards the beginning of the last century the noted vegetarian George Bernard Shaw received an invitation to the Vegetarian Society's annual dinner. He turned it down flat, claiming that the idea of 2,000 people all crunching celery at the same time simply appalled him. Well, vegetarian cookery in this country today has come a long way from crunching celery, having embraced the most wonderful dishes from right around the globe. In fact, vegetarianism today is so far from the hair-shirted Puritanism of old that a recent customer survey at Henderson's revealed that less than 10% of the regulars were actually vegetarian – the rest just loved the food!

⇨ The above information is reprinted with kind permission from Henderson's of Edinburgh. Visit www.hendersonsofedinburgh.co.uk for more information.

Why vegetarian?

The five main reasons why some people decide to follow a vegetarian lifestyle, from the Vegetarian & Vegan Foundation.

Health and nutrition

People who eat plenty of fruit and vegetables, pulses – all types of peas, beans and lentils – and whole grains (oats, wholemeal bread, whole-grain spaghetti, brown rice, etc.) but little animal fat and animal protein cut their risk of many illnesses and diseases including some of the most common cancers, heart disease, strokes, obesity and diabetes.

Protecting animals

55 billion animals are killed ever year for meat production; nearly one billion of these are slaughtered in the UK. Most of the animals raised for meat production in the UK are factory farmed, the most intensively reared being pigs, chickens, ducks and turkeys.

The environment

More than 70 per cent of all agricultural land in Britain is used to feed animals because of animal farming's inefficiency. It can take as much as 17kg of vegetable protein to produce 1kg of meat protein. The United Nations recognises that farmed animals (livestock) are the second biggest source of greenhouse gases, the main cause of deforestation and plant and animal extinctions (loss of biodiversity) and many other environmental problems.

World hunger

Over 950 million people in the world go hungry. One child dies every five seconds of hunger-related causes. One major reason is because much of the best agricultural land in the developing world is used to grow animal feed (fodder) to feed to farmed animals in rich countries or to graze animals which are killed for meat for the same affluent countries.

55 billion animals are killed ever year for meat production; nearly one billion of these are slaughtered in the UK

Religious and ethical food choices

Throughout history, some religions have required their followers to observe strict dietary guidelines, including avoiding some meat and animal products.

⇨ The above information is reprinted with kind permission from the Vegetarian and Vegan Foundation. Visit www.teachvegetarian.com for more information.

Vegetarianism: ethics and religion

A short explanation of what each religion teaches about eating animals as food.

Buddhism

There are five founding beliefs or precepts in Buddhism. The first one is not killing or causing harm to other living beings. Therefore many Buddhists follow a vegetarian (or vegan) diet. However, many don't. Like most religions, there is often a difference between Buddhist principles (rules and beliefs) and Buddhist practice – what people actually do in their lives! For example, Tibetan Buddhists are often meat eaters, partly because growing plant foods is difficult in the country's harsh climate – and partly because of tradition. In some countries, Buddhist monks are given alms (food) by householders and are supposed to take what is given, so are permitted to eat meat in food given to them. Buddhists in India are more likely to be vegetarian.

Christianity

Most Christian churches do not teach vegetarianism and many Christians believe that humans are appointed by God as 'stewards' of the Earth. However, many early Christians are believed to have been vegetarian. Today, the Seventh Day Adventist Church teaches vegetarianism as a general rule and there are also many other Christians who go vegetarian for such reasons as feeding the world, the environment and factory farming – or who just believe we should protect animals and the Earth from harm, not exploit them.

Hinduism

Many Hindus are vegetarian due to their belief in non-violence (*ahimsa*). The Hindu religion also believes that the soul inside the body of an animal is similar to that of a soul in a human body – another reason for not eating animals.

Judaism

While many Jews continue to eat meat, Jewish ritual slaughter rules were introduced originally to reduce the suffering of animals being killed for meat. However, many Jews now opt for a completely or partially vegetarian diet because they are against factory farming and cruelty in general.

Rastafarianism

Rastafari is a religion based in Jamaica. Its followers believe in the teachings of Haile Selassie I, the last Emperor of Ethiopia, whom they worship as an incarnation of Jah, or God. Many Rastafarians follow an I-tal diet, a type of vegan diet. Others may abstain from eating pork or certain foodstuffs but are not strictly vegetarian.

Sikhism

Sikhs are free to choose whether to adopt a vegetarian diet or meat-eating diet. Sikhism is a liberal, tolerant faith that acknowledges personal liberty and free will. This faith offers spiritual, ethical and moral guidance to a fulfilling way of life rather than a list of strict rules.

Other religions

Religions such as Judaism, Christianity and Islam do not promote vegetarianism, but do not discount it as a way of life. In fact, groups such as The Catholic (Christian) Vegetarian Society believe that vegetarianism complements their religion. There are also significant numbers of Jewish vegetarians.

Can you follow your religion and be vegetarian?

Vegetarianism does not get in the way of religious beliefs; in fact, it is possible to eat Halal and Kosher while maintaining a vegetarian lifestyle. Some Jews and Muslims are vegetarian to prevent religious slaughter which they believe to be cruel because the animals are conscious throughout.

Ethics without religion

Some people do not follow a religion, but nonetheless try to live in an ethical way, e.g. Humanists or other atheists. They may be against eating meat because they believe that it is wrong to take a life. Many people find it hard to justify an animal's death simply for taste; because humans do not need meat to live they regard killing animals as cruel and unnecessary.

⇨ The above information is an extract from *The Right Stuff? Ethics and Religion* and is reprinted with kind permission from the Vegetarian and Vegan Foundation. Visit www.teachvegetarian.com for more information on this and other related topics.

VEGETARIAN AND VEGAN FOUNDATION

Don't call it vegetarian, it is 'meat free'

Retailers are increasingly selling dishes as 'meat free' as vegetarianism is seen as 'outdated' and unfashionable.

By Alastair Jamieson

Vegetarian food has moved a long way since the infamous nut roast and the lentil burger. But now it has run into a new problem – the name.

Supermarkets are dropping the prominent use of the word 'vegetarian' from new meat-free dishes because they fear it puts off modern health-conscious eaters.

Worse still for those still committed to the cause, the new 'meat-free' dishes are being sold in the same aisles as meals made from pork and beef.

Retail analysts said the stores were trying to distance themselves from the 'negative or outdated connotations' of vegetarianism.

Vegetarians admitted that they were no longer 'this year's flavour' but criticised the level of 'commitment' of modern shoppers.

Supermarkets are dropping the prominent use of the word 'vegetarian' from new meat-free dishes because they fear it puts off modern health-conscious eaters

Marks & Spencer is the latest supermarket to launch a range of ready meals suitable for vegetarians but sold alongside staples such as chicken curry or pork medallions.

Rather than being prominently displayed, the word 'vegetarian' is confined to small print on the corner of the packaging.

'Certain customers would not shop in a vegetarian section as they are not vegetarian, in the same way that the average customer would not shop for gluten or wheat free unless they had an intolerance,' said Lesley Anderson, health meals developer for M&S.

She added meat-free dishes were 'quite fashionable', boosted by Nigel Slater's book *Tender: A Cook and his Vegetable Patch* and Sir Paul McCartney's Meat-Free Mondays campaign.

'Vegetarians are only about six per cent of the market so we obviously want to open it out to the whole population,' she said.

The store has shrunk the size of its dedicated vegetarian section in recent years.

The meat-free trend has been boosted by United Nations climate change reports calling for a global shift towards a plant-based diet to reduce greenhouse gas emissions from farm animals and make world food supplies more sustainable.

Asda also uses the 'meat-free' tag on a range of ready meals, but these are stocked on a separate shelf from those containing meat. Sainsbury's has stocked some tinned items with the 'meat-free' label.

The high cost of meat and the health benefits from eating more vegetables have pushed up annual sales of meat-free ready meals such as risotto or bean burgers by one fifth over the past five years to £553m.

Research by Mintel shows the number of consumers calling themselves 'vegetarian' has stuck stubbornly for the past five years at about six per cent of the overall food market.

However, the number who agree with the statement 'I eat meat-free foods' is about 60 per cent.

Kiti Soininen, senior food and drink analyst at Mintel, said: 'The top reasons why people choose meat free are for variety, because they are healthier, it is a lighter meal or because it looks tasty.

'Ethical reasons are really low among those consumers.

'It doesn't seem to be about "I want to save the animals", it is more about "better for me".'

She added: 'Within the industry there seems to have been a shift, rather than highlighting the "vegetarian" term very strongly on packaging, there has tended to be a shift towards talk about "meat free" because it would seem the term vegetarian has got slightly negative or outdated connotations.

'To put it strongly, it is denying yourself something by being vegetarian whereas by being meat free it has more positive connotations of being good to yourself and going with the push for healthier eating.'

The shifting trend has frustrated some vegetarians, who fear it will become harder to find dishes that are completely free of animal products such as gelatin or Parmesan cheese.

Liz O'Neill, head of communications at the Vegetarian Society, said: 'We're definitely not this year's flavour.

THE TELEGRAPH

Commitment is not very fashionable. I think it is sad as something fundamental is being lost.

'I'm thrilled and delighted that so many people are recognising the value of eating less meat but it is not the same as being vegetarian.

'It doesn't involve the same commitment and there's a real issue about people wanting to have their cake and eat it.'

She added: 'There seems to be a strong personal choice agenda. By going for this blander, meat-free brand you are actually making choice much harder for vegetarians if they have to make that commitment because it is harder to find what is suitable.

'If any supermarket puts their meat-free brand in a fridge alongside the meat, vegetarians might not walk down that aisle. We all have our familiar routes in the supermarket.'

The new M&S range of 'Lovely Vegetables' meals includes Beetroot & Goats Cheese Risotto and Roasted Butternut Squash and Chargrilled Halloumi.

Eight of the nine microwaveable dishes are suitable for vegetarians while the other contained fish sauce.

M&S said it would continue to stock a large range of vegetarian products, including ready meals.

16 January 2011

Meat-free foods

Report brochure from Mintel.

What is *Meat-free foods* about?

Three in five UK adults now eat meat-free food, according to consumer research for this report. However, only six per cent of adults identify themselves as vegetarians, this share remaining broadly stagnant in recent years. Demand from people eating both meat and meat-free foods has been a key factor supporting underlying growth in the market, driven, for example, by the quest for variety and health considerations.

The consumer research for this report shows considerable openness among mainstream consumers to meat-free food if it delivers as a culinary experience, with nearly half of adults saying they would consider such food if it was tasty or exciting in its own right. Supporting this finding, the quest for variety stands out as the most popular reason for eating meat-free or vegetarian foods.

What have we found out?

- Products bringing diversity to the mainstream meat-free offering stand to find demand among the 11 million adults who say they would eat meat-free food more, given greater variety.
- The ready and ready-to-cook meal sectors could benefit from broadening their meat-free offering, to cater for the 12 million adults that think there aren't enough meat-free options in these categories.
- Over three million 16- to 34-year-olds would like to cut back on meat/fish/poultry, a potentially lucrative target for meat-free foods that can facilitate this within their established cooking habits.
- Traditional and natural high-protein ingredients like tempeh or quinoa could spark interest among the nearly seven million ABs [the NRS social grade classification which refers to those in higher and intermediate managerial, administrative or professional careers] who report being put off by meat substitutes because they see these as artificial or processed.
- Meat-free foods drawing inspiration from ethnic cuisines could spark interest among the four million 25- to 34-year-olds who would consider vegetarian or meat-free food if it was exciting or tasty in its own right, this age group also being top users of ethnic foods.
- Delivering on all around healthiness, such as low fat and calories, could help meat-free foods increase their appeal to the nearly seven million adults who choose such foods when wanting a lighter meal.

December 2010

- The above information is reprinted with kind permission from Mintel. Visit www.mintel.com for more information.

THE TELEGRAPH / MINTEL

The health benefits of eating Quorn products

You may know Quorn as a range of foods popular with vegetarians. What you may not know is that more and more non-vegetarians are incorporating Quorn products into their diets to help them follow a lighter, healthier lifestyle. Information from Marlow Foods, the manufacturers of Quorn.

What is Quorn?

Quorn is the brand name for a versatile range of healthy foods. At the heart of all Quorn products is a unique ingredient called mycoprotein.

Mycoprotein is made from a nutritious member of the fungi family which was discovered growing in a garden in Marlow, Buckinghamshire 40 years ago.

Today there are more than 100 products in the Quorn range, from burgers and sausages to ready meals and pies.

Here we focus on the cooking ingredients in the range, Quorn Mince and Quorn Pieces, both of which are very high in mycoprotein.

What are the benefits of replacing meat with Quorn Mince and Quorn Pieces?

Like meat, Quorn Mince and Quorn Pieces are excellent sources of protein but they're generally lower in saturated fat and calories than their meat equivalents. For example, Quorn Mince contains only 54 per cent of the calories of beef mince, about 22 per cent of the fat, and just 14 per cent of the saturates. Quorn Mince and Quorn Pieces also contain no cholesterol and no trans fats at all. They're also good sources of dietary fibre. In fact you get more fibre from 100g of Quorn Mince than from 100g of baked beans. By the way, there is no dietary fibre at all in meat and poultry.

Health benefits of Quorn products

There have been a number of academic studies examining the health properties of mycoprotein, the special ingredient in all Quorn products.

Cholesterol

Most Quorn products contain no cholesterol, but in addition to that research suggests that mycoprotein may have a valuable role to play in helping to maintain healthy cholesterol levels or even to lower LDL (bad) cholesterol, so helping to maintain a healthy heart.

Weight control

There is also evidence to suggest that mycoprotein can help improve what dieticians call 'satiety', the sense of feeling satisfied and full. Hence, mycoprotein may help regulate energy intake among those looking to control or lose weight.

Do Quorn products have all the same nutrients as meat and poultry?

Quorn products have less of the things that most people need to cut down on, such as fat, saturates and calories. But broadly speaking, you can get all the good things from Quorn products that you get from meat. In fact, the quality of protein in Quorn Mince and Quorn Pieces is identical to chicken and a little better than beef. Being vegetable in origin, there is less iron in Quorn products than in red meat but this can be made up with foods such as leafy green vegetables, lentils, kidney beans and some dried fruits.

How do I cook with Quorn products?

In general, Quorn foods can be prepared using a conventional oven or microwave. They can be prepared in a similar fashion to their meat and poultry counterparts. They're delicious and tasty grilled, baked and sautéed, and can be prepared quickly and easily, and there's no pre-preparation necessary and no waste. Cooking instructions appear on each pack and will of course vary depending on the product type.

Where can I get more information about Quorn products?

For more information about Quorn visit www.quorn.co.uk. For more information about mycoprotein visit www.mycoprotein.org

⇨ The above information is reprinted with kind permission from Marlow Foods. Visit www.mycoprotein.org for more information.

MARLOW FOODS

Vegetarians are 'not happy' with food, says new research

Information from MMR Research Worldwide Ltd.

A new study of just under 6,000 UK consumers by MMR Research Worldwide reveals that the majority of vegetarians supplement their diet – 25% are 'not satisfied' with vegetarian food ranges in supermarkets, while 76% are unimpressed with fast food restaurants.

The findings include the following statistics:

- 10% of lapsed vegetarians have moved away from a vegetarian lifestyle primarily due to concerns over health and nutrition.
- The majority of UK vegetarians feel the need to supplement their diet with vitamins and minerals.
- Around a quarter of vegetarians are not satisfied with the choice of vegetarian options available to them in their supermarket.
- 76% of vegetarians are not happy with the choice available to them in fast food restaurants.

Research from food and drink research specialists MMR Research Worldwide for National Vegetarian Week 2010 (24–30 May) has found that concern over the nutritional benefit of a vegetarian diet is turning vegetarians to dietary supplements, and in some cases even back to meat.

Furthermore, supermarkets are failing to satisfy about a quarter of vegetarians with ready meals, frozen foods and meat substitute products. MMR, which advises leading food brands on product development by conducting consumer and sensory research, urges companies to address issues faced by the vegetarian market as well as the market of 'reluctant meat eaters' to maximise revenue.

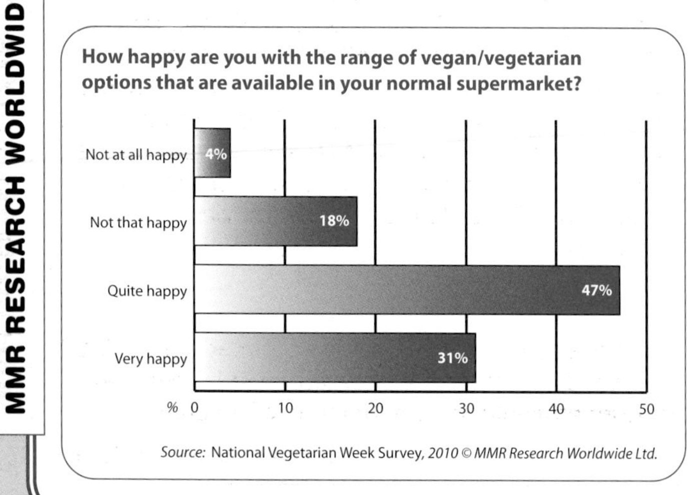

Source: National Vegetarian Week Survey, *2010 © MMR Research Worldwide Ltd.*

Vegetarians are 27% more likely to buy vitamin and mineral supplements than non-vegetarians. With 50% of the vegetarian sample of 357 regularly taking vitamin supplements (compared with 36% of the 5,582 non-vegetarians) and 26% taking mineral supplements (compared with 15% of non-vegetarians), the majority of UK vegetarians are feeling the need to supplement their diet.

'Sales of dietary supplements and fortified food could be increased if brands adopted more targeted marketing towards vegetarian consumers who are more likely to be receptive to nutritional benefit messages,' says Mat Lintern, MD of MMR Research Worldwide. 'Interestingly, lapsed vegetarians – representing a surprisingly large 10% of our sample – cite concerns over health and nutrition as a reason for eventually returning to meat. So, it might even be the case that more consumers would convert to vegetarianism if they were suitably educated about the role of a range of vegetarian food products and/or fortified foods in maintaining a healthy, meat-free diet.'

Opportunity for supermarkets

An issue for the UK's grocery giants is the fact that 22% of vegetarians were not satisfied with the choice of vegetarian options available to them in their supermarket. The problem is much more acute in convenience stores, and less than half of the vegetarians polled were happy with the choice available.

'Almost 25% of consumers call for a dedicated supermarket section in-store, with a similar proportion stating they would like to see a wider choice of meat substitute products,' says Lintern. 'There's a huge opportunity for the likes of Tesco Express, Co-op and Spar to do more in terms of widening their vegetarian ranges and making sure they're visible on the shelves. Our survey revealed that plenty of non-vegetarians opt for vegetarian meals, so these products should be appealing to all consumers.'

More than three-quarters of vegetarians are not happy with the choice of foods available to them in fast food restaurants. Only 3% were very happy with the choice. Pubs and restaurants fare better: almost half were happy with the choice, yet still with a considerable opportunity to better satisfy the vegetarian market.

The MMR Research Worldwide study provides a range

MMR RESEARCH WORLDWIDE LTD

of insights from UK vegetarians and vegans relevant to food brands. As may be expected, vegetarians are more likely to choose healthy products provided they're quick to prepare.

They are motivated by products with no artificial ingredients and are less likely to buy ready meals because of health concerns. They are keen on ethical and quality food and attribute more importance than non-vegetarians to issues of free range and animal welfare, recyclable packaging, sustainable production, fair trade, carbon neutral, food miles, natural, low fat, whole grain and organic.

Being health-aware

Meat substitute products: over 90% of vegetarians buy meat substitutes, and the ones that don't cite not liking the taste or texture. Over a third eat them most days, and this figure rises to almost 80% among vegans. The quality of meat substitute products is generally regarded as 'good/acceptable', with 69% awarding them a seven or more on a ten-point opinion scale.

Dairy products: while 85% are happy with vegetarian product labelling, cheese and yogurts were the only products mentioned by more than a handful of people as being a problem in this regard.

'On average, the typical vegetarian is just a little more health-aware when it comes to food, which obviously has implications for the food that's produced for them and how it's packaged and marketed,' says Lintern. 'They are also more likely to be reading ingredients labels than non-vegetarians, which suggests the importance of product labelling to indicate suitability for vegetarians. Finally, companies wishing to target vegetarians are advised to link their products with environmental, ethical and fair trade messages.'

25 May 2010

⇨ The above information is reprinted with kind permission from MMR Research Worldwide Ltd, accessed via www.foodbev.com

Appearance matters more than taste for meat substitutes

Information from Next Generation Food.

If it's true that you eat with your eyes, then meat substitutes may be in for a rough time, according to a new study. Researchers in the Netherlands found that the appearance of meat substitutes in a meal may have more of an effect on consumer acceptance than flavour and texture.

Researchers set out to investigate the role of meal context on the acceptance of meat substitutes. They focused on Quorn pieces and mince (mycoprotein and egg white), tofu strips (soy bean curd and olive oil), Tivall stir fry pieces (soy, egg and pea proteins, vegetable oil), Goodbite chicken style (soy, egg and wheat proteins), and Vivera vega stir fry pieces (soy protein and olive oil).

A total of 93 participants were recruited in the Wageningen area of the Netherlands. Vegetarians and people with allergies to any of the replacements were excluded, while participants had varying levels of meat consumption. In general, the use of meat substitutes amongst this group was low.

On ten days within a two- week period, the participants attended a central location and took part in two tests. The first assessed the role of appropriateness and meal context on acceptance: meat substitutes of the same brand and constitution, but with a different shape and appearance (pieces versus mince) were served in four different meal concepts (rice, spaghetti, soup and salad). Participants' appropriateness, positive reaction and intention to use the meat substitute before and after tasting were assessed.

The researchers found that acceptance of meat substitutes was influenced by the overall meat concept, and appropriateness of a meat substitute in a meal as rated before tasting tended to influence acceptance of the meal.

'For meat substitutes to be accepted by non-vegetarian consumers, the shape and appearance was important,' said the report. 'The ingredients, flavour and texture of the meat substitutes did not seem to be crucial for the acceptance of meals with meat substitutes.'

Meat consumption has come under the spotlight in recent times, as excessive consumption of meat, especially red meat, has been linked to increased risk of various cancers and other lifestyle diseases. In addition, high demand for animal-derived proteins is adding to climate change and sustainability concerns. Some countries, such as Sweden and Germany, have incorporated environmental advice on meat eating into dietary guidelines alongside health advice.

1 June 2011

⇨ The above information is reprinted with kind permission from Next Generation Food. Visit www.nextgenerationfood.com for more information.

Being veggie: frequently asked questions

Information from The Vegetarian Society of the United Kingdom Ltd.

Once you have made the choice to go veggie, it's likely that friends and family members (even non-friends and non-family!) will constantly ask you why. Some will delight in trying to dissuade you from your choice. They may also ask you challenging questions in an effort to make you question your decision. Don't be intimidated! Feel confident in knowing you have made a positive, healthy, ethical decision – one that is good for you, good for the animals, and good for the environment. One of the most annoying things about being a veggie is being asked the same questions over and over again!

Here are some of the most commonly asked questions and some suggested answers.

Isn't vegetarianism unhealthy?

Vegetarianism is a healthy choice as long as a wide range of foods is eaten. Chocolate and chips are vegetarian: however, they do not represent a balanced diet. Research comparing a balanced meat diet to a balanced veggie diet found that the vegetarian diet was the healthiest (The Oxford Vegetarian Study).

Isn't protein only available from meat?

Protein is available in all foods apart from refined white sugar and some oils and your protein needs are automatically met by a balanced, varied diet. Meat does provide protein: however, it is only one source. Nuts, beans, eggs, soya, textured vegetable protein, Quorn and lentils are all excellent sources of protein.

Isn't eating meat natural?

Arguing that an action is natural can be quite problematic. A common argument used by meat eaters is that because we have canine teeth this is evidence that we have been 'designed' to eat meat. Along with sharp claws, all meat eaters, since they have to kill mainly with their teeth, possess powerful jaws and pointed, elongated, 'canine' teeth to pierce tough skin and to spear and tear flesh. They do NOT have flat, back teeth like us which vegetarian animals need for grinding their food. As for our sharp teeth, gorillas are entirely vegetarian – as are almost all primates – and yet have far longer and sharper canine teeth than human beings!

Isn't vegetarian food more expensive than meat dishes?

Pre-packaged foods (ready meals) are expensive whether they are vegetarian or meat-based. Vegetarian dishes in restaurants tend to be lower priced than most meat dishes, and preparing vegetarian food from scratch at home can be very inexpensive. As is true with cooking non-veggie food, the cost all depends on the ingredients you choose and the quality of the products you buy.

THE VEGETARIAN SOCIETY OF THE UNITED KINGDOM LTD

Doesn't cooking vegetarian food take a long time?

Just as in meat-based cooking, there are some veggie dishes that take a long time to prepare and there are others that are super-quick. It all depends on what you are in the mood for and how much time you have on your hands.

If you're a vegetarian, why are you wearing leather shoes?

First of all, it may be the case that your shoes are not made of leather; they just look like they are. There are lots of vegetarian shoes on the market these days. Secondly, many vegetarians have leather products from their pre-veggie days and have made the choice to continue wearing them rather than have them go to waste. There are also some people who are not comfortable eating meat, yet continue wearing leather. It is a question of where you as an individual choose to draw a line. Of course, if you are not comfortable with an animal dying for your dinner, you probably aren't comfortable with them dying for your clothes and footwear either.

You will find vegetarians amongst the followers of all the major religions, including Christianity, Islam, Buddhism, Judaism and Hinduism

Don't fruit and vegetables have feelings and feel pain when they're picked and eaten?

No! Fruit and vegetables do not have nervous systems that are similar to humans and animals and are therefore unable to feel pain.

Don't some religions suggest that it's alright to eat animals?

Nearly a quarter of the world's population enjoys a vegetarian diet and you will find vegetarians amongst the followers of all the major religions, including Christianity, Islam, Buddhism, Judaism and Hinduism. Many religions demand specific practices in the preparation and eating of different foods and these are open to differing interpretations; however, it is possible to observe any of these requirements whilst following a vegetarian diet without compromising any religious belief.

What's the point of going veggie if everyone else keeps eating meat?

Most people go veggie because they don't think it's right or necessary to eat animals for our food. The average vegetarian saves the lives of over 50 land animals and hundreds of fish each year. That sounds like a very good reason for going veggie to me!

People also choose to go veggie as it's more healthy for them and because by giving up meat they make less impact on the environment and the planet's resources.

It's important for everyone to make their own decisions about lots of things and no-one should ever feel as though they have to do something just because everyone else is. Things would never get better if that happened! And not everyone else is eating meat anyway – nearly a quarter of the world's population enjoy a veggie diet! Maybe if other people see how easy and healthy it is to go veggie, they may decide to change their diet too!

⇨ The above information is reprinted with kind permission from The Vegetarian Society of the United Kingdom Ltd. Visit www.vegsoc.org and www.youngveggie.org for more information.

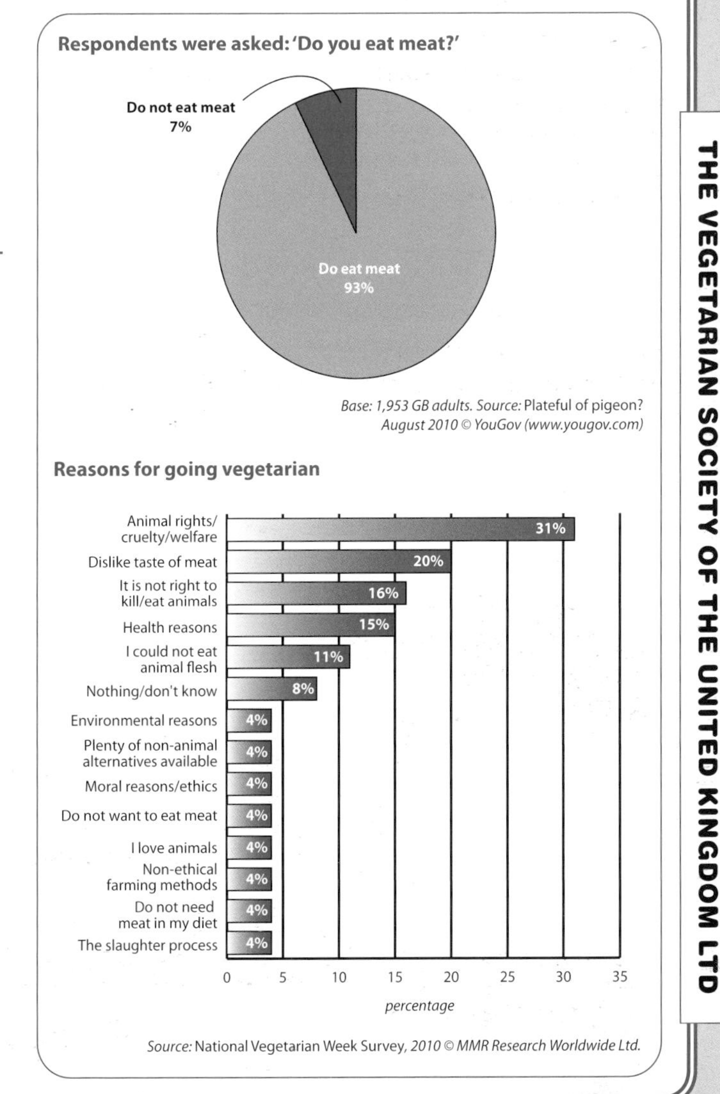

THE VEGETARIAN SOCIETY OF THE UNITED KINGDOM LTD

Why I stopped being a vegetarian

To be vegetarian is to be a pacifist, avoiding the fight against animal cruelty. Eat meat from sustainable farms, and we will win.

By Jenna Woginrich

I was a vegetarian for a long time – the bulk of my adult life, actually. When I realised how most of the steaks got to my plate (and how pumped full of antibiotics and growth hormones they were), I put down my fork and took a vow to never be a part of that system again. My research into the brutal American factory farm system and its effects on the environment was a life-changing stumble down into the rabbit hole; I discovered a twisted world of assembly-line death camps, crippled animals, radiated carcasses and festering diseases. I don't have to get into the specifics, but clearly it wasn't a compassionate way to get my suggested 46 grams of protein a day. So I stopped eating meat, cold Tofurkey.

Nearly a decade later I'm no longer a vegetarian. In fact, I couldn't be further from the produce aisle. Nowadays I own and operate a small farm where I raise my own chicken, pork, lamb, rabbit, turkey and eggs. I had a serious change of heart, and it happened when I realised my aversion to meat wasn't solving the animal welfare problem I was protesting about. My beef, after all, wasn't with beef. It was with how the cow got to my plate in the first place. One way to make sure the animals I ate lived a happy, respectable life was to raise them myself. I would learn to butcher a free-range chicken, raise a pig without antibiotics and rear lambs on green hillside pastures. I would come back to meat eating, and I would do it because of my love for animals.

Every meal you eat that supports a sustainable farm changes the agricultural world. I cannot possibly stress this enough. Your fork is your ballot, and when you vote to eat a steak or leg of lamb purchased from a small farmer you are showing the industrial system you are actively opting out. You are showing them you are willing to sacrifice more of your wages to dine with dignity. As people are made more aware of this beautiful option, farmers are coming out in droves to meet the demand. Farmers markets have been on a rapid rise in the US thanks to consumer demand for cleaner meat, up 16% in the last year alone.

It's a hard reality for a vegetarian to swallow, but my veggie burgers did not rattle the industry cages at all. I was simply avoiding the battlefield, stepping aside as a pacifist. There is nobility in the vegetarian choice, but it isn't changing the system fast enough. In a world where meat consumption is soaring, the plausible 25% of the world's inhabitants who have a mostly vegetarian diet aren't making a dent in the rate us humans are eating animals. In theory, a plant-based diet avoids consuming animals but it certainly isn't getting cows out of feedlots. However, steak-eating consumers choosing to eat sustainably-raised meat are. They chose to purchase a product raised on pasture when they could have spent less money on an animal treated like a screwdriver.

I realised my aversion to meat wasn't solving the animal welfare problem I was protesting about

'There is a fundamental difference between cows and screwdrivers. Cows feel pain and screwdrivers do not.' Those are the words of Temple Grandin, the famed advocate responsible for making the meat industry aware of animal suffering. But how many of us consumers think of that steak in the plastic wrap next to the breakfast cereal and laundry detergent as just another object? A product as characterless as a screwdriver? We seem to be caught in a parted sea of extremes when it comes to how we see food – either we're adamant about where our food comes from, or completely oblivious. I don't think the world needs to convert into a society of vegans or sustainable farmers, but we do need to live in a world where beef doesn't just mean an ingredient; it means a life loss. I never thought of my beans or houmous like that. Now every meal is seasoned with the gratitude of sacrifice. For me, it took a return to carnivory to live out the ideals of vegetarianism. Food is a complicated religion.

It may mean spending more money, but the way small farmers raise their sheep, goats, cattle and hogs on pasture is the polar opposite of those cruel places where animals are treated like a cheap protein and 'quality' is a measure of economic algorithms, not life. If cruelty is bad for business, business will simply have to change. When consumers demand a higher quality of life from the animals they eat, feedlots will become a black stain of our agricultural past.

I'm sorry, my vegetarian friends, but it's time to come back to the table. You can remain in the rabbit hole and keep eating your salad, but the only way out for good is to eat the rabbit.

19 January 2011

THE GUARDIAN

Chapter 2 VEGETARIANISM AND THE ENVIRONMENT

Healthy planet eating

How lower-meat diets can save lives and the planet.

Introduction

Meat and dairy products form the centrepiece of most meals in the UK. Factory-style production and heavy subsidies have made them plentiful and cheap in Europe and America.

Our increasing consumption – of meat in particular – is prompting concern over the impacts on people's health and on the environment. But calls for changes to diets and farming methods have tended to produce a polarised and often ill-informed debate.

This report aims to throw fresh light on the stalemate. It does so by presenting evidence on the health benefits of switching to lower-meat diets.

A cultural challenge

There is little doubt about the science. In the West we eat far more meat than is necessary or healthy. Health experts say this is contributing to rising levels of chronic diseases such as coronary heart disease, cancers and strokes.

Such findings have led to calls for nutritional advice to be revised to encourage a reduction in total meat intake and discourage meat and dairy that is high in fat – particularly saturated fat – and salt. Instead, small amounts of better-quality fresh lean meat would be recommended.

Yet such thinking is not reflected in any UK Government guidelines or advice on healthy eating. Changing our concept of an average healthy diet is proving a challenge.

In the UK there tends to be an all-or-nothing approach to meat eating, with little recognition or understanding of the concept of a low-meat diet. It's telling that, while people who eat no meat are identified and identifiable – as vegetarians – there is no commonly accepted term for people who eat meat only a few times a week.

Attempts to raise awareness of the benefits of lower-meat diets and to change diets have proved controversial.

Key findings

- Over the last 50 years the quantity of meat produced around the world has quadrupled while the global population has doubled.
- We could prevent 45,000 early deaths and save the NHS £1.2 billion each year if we switched to diets that contain less meat in the UK.
- Lower-meat diets could cut deaths from heart disease by 31,000, deaths from cancer by 9,000 and deaths from strokes by 5,000 each year.
- There is clear evidence of a link between high-meat diets and a higher incidence of bowel cancer and heart disease, with some evidence of a link between high-meat diets and other cancers, diabetes and obesity.
- Processed meat is more damaging to health than unprocessed meats.
- Grass-fed beef has nutritional advantages over grain-fed options.
- The nutritional value of some meat has decreased as a result of modern farming methods. A standard supermarket chicken now contains significantly less protein and more than twice as much fat as in 1970.

In the media the issue has been oversimplified and distorted.

For example, in October 2009, climate change expert Lord Stern observed that the environmental impact of a meat diet was higher than that of a vegetarian diet. His comment was interpreted in reports as 'people will need to turn vegetarian if the world is to conquer climate change'.

Similarly, in January 2009, a plan to reduce the amount of meat served in hospitals to healthier and more sustainable levels was included in an NHS carbon-

FRIENDS OF THE EARTH

reduction strategy. The proposal focussed on reducing meat, rather than cutting it out entirely, and sourcing local produce, but was reported as a 'removal' and a 'ban' on meat and was criticised in the media. The plan was subsequently scrapped.

Ironically, we are more prepared than ever to throw meat away. Historically regarded as an indicator of affluence and, for many, a treat, meat is now artificially cheap and plentiful. The growing quantities wasted suggest that, along with other food groups, meat has become a throwaway commodity. So our attitudes towards meat are complex. What is clear is the damage that increasing consumption is doing to the environment and people.

Environmental and social damage

Meat and dairy production – now responsible for a fifth of global greenhouse gas emissions – is predicted to double by 2050. This is incompatible with the need to cut emissions by at least 80 per cent in the same period to prevent the worst effects of climate change.

Attempts to raise awareness of the benefits of lower-meat diets and to change diets have proved controversial

UK factory farms are also driving deforestation and ruining lives overseas. Vast areas of forest and wildlife in South America are being cleared to grow the protein needed to quickly bulk up millions of animals each year. This is forcing local people off their lands and into hunger and poverty.

An alternative

There is already evidence that consuming less meat would be good for the environment and would help feed a growing population.

In 2009, Friends of the Earth and Compassion in World Farming published *Eating the Planet?*, a groundbreaking report which demonstrated that we can feed a growing global population without destroying the world's natural resources or relying on factory farms – and we don't need to give up meat.

The modelling in *Eating the Planet?* showed that by adjusting our diets we could feed a global population predicted to be nine billion by 2050. Rearing animals for food uses far more land, energy and water than growing crops to provide people with the same number of calories. A diet containing no more than three portions of meat each week would take pressure off the land and the climate.

The diet outlined in *Eating the Planet?* would mean a significant reduction in meat eating in the West, yet it would allow for more meat to be eaten in developing countries where there are high levels of malnutrition. There are as many obese people in the West as there are malnourished people in poorer countries: the health and justice arguments for changes to food production and distribution are as compelling as the environmental imperatives.

This report adds to the evidence by presenting modelling on the impact of a lower-meat diet on people's health and NHS budgets. It also reviews:

- evidence of the health impacts of high meat and dairy consumption;
- the difference between good and bad meat;
- examples of healthy alternative eating advice and plans.

Eating less meat is not a silver bullet that will deliver healthy eating and living. But a growing body of evidence shows that we should get the majority of our nutrients from fresh fruits and vegetables, whole grains and pulses, with only small amounts of meat, dairy and fish as additional sources of protein. Recommendations on fish consumption when stocks are under threat are beyond the scope of this report but are covered by Greenpeace and Sustain.

Such a diet has many benefits, including:

- reducing the livestock industry's environmental impact – including on climate change;
- improving the health and well-being of people in the UK, and indeed the rest of the world;
- reducing the burden of diet-related disease on the NHS;
- helping to create a thriving and planet-friendly UK farming sector.

This report sets out what the Government needs to do to encourage healthy and sustainable diets and food production.

Grasping these opportunities would transform the UK into a model for healthy, sustainable food production and consumption that, if adopted by the rest of the world, would help ensure a fair share of the world's food resources for everyone.

October 2010

➪ The above information is an extract from Friends of the Earth's report *Healthy planet eating*, and is reprinted with permission. Visit www.foe.co.uk for more information.

FRIENDS OF THE EARTH

Going veggie... for the environment

Why going vegetarian for the environment is a positive choice.

There are many good reasons for going vegetarian. Over two million farm animals are slaughtered for food every day in the UK alone.

A balanced vegetarian diet includes all the nutrients you need to stay on top form and vegetarians have absolutely no trouble eating the recommended five portions of fruit and vegetables a day.

But what about the environment? Studies estimate that a meat-based diet requires up to three times as many resources as a vegetarian diet and here are the reasons why.

Land use and sustainability

The number of hungry people in the world is rising and, put simply, livestock farming is inefficient. Animals need to eat. In fact, they consume more than half the wheat and 60% of the barley grown in the UK and around 90% of the world's soya harvest.

They also need to breathe, move around, grow and reproduce and all of that uses up most of the energy and nutrition in the food they eat. Cattle consume around 7kg of grain for every 1kg of beef produced when they are slaughtered; pigs require 4kg for every 1kg of pork.

With 30% of the Earth's entire land surface (70% of all agricultural land) used for rearing animals, this is no trivial consideration. Livestock production is responsible for 70% of the Amazon deforestation in Latin America, where the rainforest has been cleared to create new pastures.

Growing crops to feed people rather than animals uses less land, water and other resources. The amount of land needed to produce food for someone following a typical meat-based diet could feed two and a half vegetarians, or five vegans.

Water, rivers and oceans

Over a billion people across the world do not have access to clean water and two billion do not have proper sanitation. Farming accounts for around 70% of all fresh water taken from lakes, waterways and underground water supplies, much of it to produce meat. It takes around 1–2,000 litres of water to produce a kilo of wheat and somewhere between 13,000 litres and 100,000 litres for a kilo of beef.

At sea, over-fishing depletes the oceans, while fishing practices cause damage to both wildlife and the sea itself. Inland waterways run with manure, antibiotics and hormones washed in from the land and all sorts of pollutants from industrial fish farms. Looking at the facts in this article makes it easy to see why so many people choose a vegetarian diet to help reduce their impact on the environment.

Climate change

Greenhouse gases (GHGs) act like the glass of a greenhouse, trapping heat from the Sun to warm up the Earth. The idea of warmer summers seems attractive to us in the UK, but even a small change in the world's overall temperature has a devastating impact, changing the weather, raising sea levels and destroying natural environments.

We all need to do more to reduce GHG emissions and one of the most effective ways to change your own impact is to stop eating meat and cut down on dairy. Farmed animals produce enormous quantities of GHGs.

One high-profile study even estimated that livestock farming is responsible for more greenhouse gas emissions than the world's entire transport system.

⇨ The above information is reprinted with kind permission from The Vegetarian Society of the United Kingdom Ltd. Visit www.vegsoc.org and www.youngveggie.org for more information on this and other related topics.

THE VEGETARIAN SOCIETY OF THE UNITED KINGDOM LTD

The case for eating meat

A book debunking the ethical claims made for vegetarianism has caused a stir among environmentalists. George Monbiot publicly changed his mind on the issue. So can we eat meat with a clean conscience? Simon Wilson reports.

By Simon Wilson

What's happened?

In his new book, a leading green campaigner has angered colleagues in the green lobby. Simon Fairlie, a former editor of *The Ecologist*, has challenged the received wisdom that farming meat is – or at any rate needs to be – a major cause of climate change. And in *Meat: A Benign Extravagance*, he offers a wealth of evidence to show that the case for a wholesale switch to vegetarianism is based on wrong assumptions, misleading assertions and statistical sleight of hand.

What's the response been like?

Pretty remarkable. Take the academic and campaigning journalist George Monbiot. Since 2002 he has argued that 'veganism is the only ethical response' to the threat posed by climate change. But this month he wrote a heartfelt *mea culpa* in the *Guardian*, warmly recommending Fairlie's 'forensic and objective' book. Such a public *volte-face* took many by surprise, given that Fairlie opens his book with an assault on Monbiot and his doctrinaire anti-meat attitudes.

What are the arguments against meat?

Rearing animals for meat eats up the available land in grain production and uses up the world's water. And that's before you factor in deforestation and pollution. Lord Stern, author of Britain's highly influential 2006 review of climate change, noted last year that 'meat is a wasteful use of water and creates a lot of greenhouse gases... It puts enormous pressure on the world's resources. A vegetarian diet is better.' The most frequently cited statistic (taken from the UN's 2006 report, *Livestock's Long Shadow*) claims the combined greenhouse gas emissions of animals reared for meat are about 18% of the world's total – more than all forms of transport put together.

How does Fairlie rebut that?

First, he says many of the most oft-cited statistics are flawed. For example, he shows that the 18% figure for animal emissions rests on allotting all Amazon deforestation to cattle. In fact it is driven mostly by land speculation and logging. It also muddles up gross and net production of nitrous oxide and methane. A more accurate figure is 10%. He also unpicks the widely repeated claim that it takes up to 100,000 litres of water to produce one kilo of beef. That statistic rests on the unlikely assumption that every drop of water that falls on pasture is consumed by the animals grazing on it.

So what's his conclusion?

His core point is that meat production, when done responsibly, is much more efficient than most people think – and it has an important part to play in an ethical, locally sourced diet. Campaigners for a vegetarian diet cite scientific research that the average ratio for the conversion of plant feed into meat is between 5:1 and 10:1 in global terms. But Fairlie argues that this figure assumes that animals only eat food that humans could eat – which is not the case. A more appropriate approach is to compare the amount of land needed to rear meat with the land required to grow plant products of the same nutritional value to humans. As such, a more accurate conversion ratio is 1.4:1.

He also unpicks the widely repeated claim that it takes up to 100,000 litres of water to produce one kilo of beef

And the implication?

Fairlie shows that if we stopped feeding edible grain to animals – in particular pigs – we could produce about half as much meat as we do with no loss to human nutrition. In fact, there would be a net gain, in global terms. For example, in many parts of the rich world pigs have been prevented from doing what comes naturally to them – converting kitchen or slaughterhouse waste into meat – largely due to a panicked over-reaction to BSE and other food scares. As a result, they often eat soya imported from the Americas – a grossly inefficient food source. If this kind of anomaly could be taken out of the meat industry, there's no reason why humans shouldn't continue to eat meat – albeit less of it, and of higher quality – in good conscience.

MONEYWEEK

Would turning vegetarian help the environment?

YES

- Humans eat about 230 million tonnes of meat a year – twice as much as we did 30 years ago. That is putting unsustainable pressure on land and water, especially as demand for meat increases as developing nations get richer.
- Chickens, cows, sheep and pigs are all vastly inefficient converters of feed and water into energy for humans, compared with plants and crops.
- Rearing animals for meat places a massive pressure on the world's grain resources and therefore increases global hunger.

NO

- Vegans (and many vegetarians) rely heavily on imported fats and proteins from distant countries. A far greener approach would be to adopt a lower-energy, lower-waste model of domestic meat production.
- No one can totally avoid foods that play a part in global warming; singling out meat is simplistic and misleading.
- A big increase in vegetarianism in Britain (which farms efficiently) would result in more meat production shifting overseas. That would increase the amount of arable land used.

24 September 2010

- The above information is reprinted with kind permission from MoneyWeek. Visit their website at www.moneyweek.com for more information on this and other related topics.

Will eating less meat save the planet?

Global warming experts warn that livestock farming produces vast amounts of greenhouse gases, and they are urging us to cut down on meat to help stem global warming. But will it really help?

What's the story?

In the war against global warming, bovine and ovine flatulence isn't an immediately obvious battlefront – but the United Nations' Food and Agriculture Organization claims that meat production accounts for nearly a fifth of global greenhouse gas emissions. This is largely because livestock emit lots of methane, which is 23 times more potent as a greenhouse gas than carbon dioxide. Some experts suggest that sticking to veg once a week would have more beneficial effects than reducing car journeys.

Cutting back on imported foods saves a huge amount of carbon dioxide emissions from transport

Who disagrees?

The Food Climate Research Network (FCRN) estimates that livestock generate only eight per cent of UK emissions, and says that eating meat is good for the planet in some ways, as some habitats benefit from grazing. The FCRN also points out that vegetarian diets that include lots of dairy products wouldn't noticeably reduce emissions.

What are the stats?

Producing a pound of beef creates the same amount of greenhouse gas as driving for 77 miles. The amount of greenhouse gas a cow produces annually is the equivalent of driving 7,800 miles. Britain eats a million tons of beef a year, 1.3 million tons of pork and 1.8 million tons of poultry, and world meat consumption is set to double in the next 20 years as developing countries become richer.

What can I do?

Consider going meat and dairy free one day a week. But if that doesn't appeal, then buy British. Cutting back on imported foods saves a huge amount of carbon dioxide emissions from transport – plus, meat production in the UK is more environmentally friendly than in many parts of the world, such as Brazil, where rainforests are bulldozed to rear cattle.

- The above information is reprinted with kind permission from *Delicious* magazine. Visit www.deliciousmagazine.co.uk for more information on this and other topics.

I was wrong about veganism. Let them eat meat – but farm it properly

The ethical case against eating animal produce once seemed clear. But a new book is an abattoir for dodgy arguments.

By George Monbiot

This will not be an easy column to write. I am about to put down 1,200 words in support of a book that starts by attacking me and often returns to this sport. But it has persuaded me that I was wrong. More to the point, it has opened my eyes to some fascinating complexities in what seemed to be a black and white case.

In the *Guardian* in 2002 I discussed the sharp rise in the number of the world's livestock, and the connection between their consumption of grain and human malnutrition. After reviewing the figures, I concluded that veganism 'is the only ethical response to what is arguably the world's most urgent social justice issue'. I still believe that the diversion of ever wider tracts of arable land from feeding people to feeding livestock is iniquitous and grotesque. So does the book I'm about to discuss. I no longer believe that the only ethical response is to stop eating meat.

In *Meat: A Benign Extravagance*, Simon Fairlie pays handsome tribute to vegans for opening up the debate. He then subjects their case to the first treatment I've read that is both objective and forensic. His book is an abattoir for misleading claims and dodgy figures, on both sides of the argument.

There's no doubt that the livestock system has gone horribly wrong. Fairlie describes the feedlot beef industry (in which animals are kept in pens) in the US as 'one of the biggest ecological cock-ups in modern history'. It pumps grain and forage from irrigated pastures into the farm animal species least able to process them efficiently, to produce beef fatty enough for hamburger production. Cattle are excellent converters of grass but terrible converters of concentrated feed. The feed would have been much better used to make pork.

Pigs, in the meantime, have been forbidden in many parts of the rich world from doing what they do best: converting waste into meat. Until the early 1990s, only 33% of compound pig feed in the UK consisted of grains fit for human consumption: the rest was made up of crop residues and food waste. Since then the proportion of sound grain in pig feed has doubled. There are several reasons: the rules set by supermarkets; the domination of the feed industry by large corporations, which can't handle waste from many different sources; but most importantly the panicked over-reaction to the BSE and foot-and-mouth crises.

Feeding meat and bone meal to cows was insane. Feeding it to pigs, whose natural diet incorporates a fair bit of meat, makes sense, as long as it is rendered properly. The same goes for swill. Giving sterilised scraps to pigs solves two problems at once: waste disposal and the diversion of grain. Instead we now dump or incinerate millions of tonnes of possible pig food and replace it with soya whose production trashes the Amazon. Waste food in the UK, Fairlie calculates, could make 800,000 tonnes of pork, or one-sixth of our total meat consumption.

THE GUARDIAN

But these idiocies, Fairlie shows, are not arguments against all meat eating, but arguments against the current farming model. He demonstrates that we've been using the wrong comparison to judge the efficiency of meat production. Instead of citing a simple conversion rate of feed into meat, we should be comparing the amount of land required to grow meat with the land needed to grow plant products of the same nutritional value to humans. The results are radically different.

If pigs are fed on residues and waste, and cattle on straw, stovers and grass from fallows and rangelands – food for which humans don't compete – meat becomes a very efficient means of food production. Even though it is tilted by the profligate use of grain in rich countries, the global average conversion ratio of useful plant food to useful meat is not the 5:1 or 10:1 cited by almost everyone, but less than 2:1. If we stopped feeding edible grain to animals, we could still produce around half the current global meat supply with no loss to human nutrition: in fact it's a significant net gain.

Waste food in the UK, Fairlie calculates, could make 800,000 tonnes of pork, or one-sixth of our total meat consumption

It's the second half – the stuffing of animals with grain to boost meat and milk consumption, mostly in the rich world – which reduces the total food supply. Cut this portion out and you would create an increase in available food which could support 1.3 billion people. Fairlie argues we could afford to use a small amount of grain for feeding livestock, allowing animals to mop up grain surpluses in good years and slaughtering them in lean ones. This would allow us to consume a bit more than half the world's current volume of animal products, which means a good deal less than in the average western diet.

He goes on to butcher a herd of sacred cows. Like many greens I have thoughtlessly repeated the claim that it requires 100,000 litres of water to produce every kilogram of beef. Fairlie shows that this figure is wrong by around three orders of magnitude. It arose from the absurd assumption that every drop of water that falls on a pasture disappears into the animals that graze it, never to re-emerge. A ridiculous amount of fossil water is used to feed cattle on irrigated crops in California, but this is a stark exception.

Similarly daft assumptions underlie the UN Food and Agriculture Organization's famous claim that livestock are responsible for 18% of the world's greenhouse gas emissions, a higher proportion than transport. Fairlie shows that it made a number of basic mistakes. It attributes all deforestation that culminates in cattle ranching in the Amazon to cattle: in reality it is mostly driven by land speculation and logging. It muddles up one-off emissions from deforestation with ongoing pollution. It makes similar boobs in its nitrous oxide and methane accounts, confusing gross and net production. (Conversely, the Organization greatly underestimates fossil fuel consumption by intensive farming: its report seems to have been informed by a powerful bias against extensive livestock keeping.)

Overall, Fairlie estimates that farmed animals produce about 10% of the world's emissions: still too much, but a good deal less than transport. He also shows that many vegetable oils have a bigger footprint than animal fats, and reminds us that even vegan farming necessitates the large-scale killing or ecological exclusion of animals: in this case pests. On the other hand, he slaughters the claims made by some livestock farmers about the soil carbon they can lock away.

The meat-producing system Fairlie advocates differs sharply from the one now practised in the rich world: low energy, low waste, just, diverse, small-scale. But if we were to adopt it, we could eat meat, milk and eggs (albeit much less) with a clean conscience. By keeping out of the debate over how livestock should be kept, those of us who have advocated veganism have allowed the champions of cruel, destructive, famine-inducing meat farming to prevail. It's time we got stuck in.

6 September 2010

THE GUARDIAN

You don't have to be vegetarian to save the planet

We can eat a diet including macaroni cheese, chicken curry and fish and chips that is good for people and the planet, argues WWF UK campaigner Duncan Williamson.

By Duncan Williamson

Food is an emotive issue. Everyone has an opinion on it, and people don't like being told that their food choices might be harming their health or the planet. Calls to change our diets have been met with howls of derision, with people misinterpreting recommendations for changes to mean that everyone should switch to a dull, grey, tasteless diet, and with polarised arguments about meat-eating versus vegetarianism.

The simple fact is that something is wrong with our global food system. One in ten of the world's population is obese, a whopping half a billion people, and hundreds of millions more are overweight. At the same time a billion people are hungry and, according to the UK Government's *Foresight* report, another billion are suffering from hidden hunger.

The food system also has a substantial impact on climate change. It is a driving force behind habitat and biodiversity loss and a huge drain on water resources, both due to the direct production of food and the growing of crops to feed animals. Around 70 per cent of all agricultural land is used to grow crops for livestock as a result of an increase in meat consumption. Agriculture on this scale requires massive amounts of water, posing an increasing threat to water-stressed areas.

Habitats under threat

Consider the production of soybean in Brazil. Vast tracts of previously untouched savannah and forest are making way for huge plantations of the crop, to feed cattle, chickens and pigs. The effects are perhaps at their most stark in Brazil's Cerrado savannah. The region – which is home to an incredible array of flora and fauna – is being cleared faster than the Amazon. The international demand for beef (and soy) has raised the value of land in the Cerrado, causing the production of beef for domestic consumption to move northwards to the Amazon rainforest.

WWF UK

Then there's palm oil, used in everything from chocolate bars and biscuits to shower gels. The tropical forests of Borneo and Sumatra, home to the endangered orang-utan, are being cleared at a rapid pace for palm oil. Elsewhere, coffee, fruit juice, wine and even olive oil are among a host of other food imports associated with significant agricultural activity affecting many areas of outstanding ecological importance.

To mitigate the effects of agriculture on habitats and protect against biodiversity loss, we therefore must change the way we consume, including what we eat. In WWF's *Living Planet Report* (2010) we called for a reduction in meat consumption and in our recent *Energy Report* (February 2011) our research clearly shows that this will only be possible if there is a reduction in meat consumption by 50 per cent in OECD countries.

The Government's recent, hugely influential, *Foresight* report also highlights, amongst other things, the need to change our diets, to eat less resource-intensive food. This change will reduce the burden the food places on nature. Making changes now will also undoubtedly benefit biodiversity, an often overlooked impact of the food system with the focus on climate change.

Livewell: sustainable diets

We believe, however, that it's possible to eat well in a way which is good for people and the planet. It's for this reason that WWF is working on sustainable diets, launching the *Livewell* report earlier this month in association with the Rowett Institute of Nutrition and Health, experts in developing healthy and specialist diets.

The *Livewell* 2020 menu contains fish and chips, macaroni cheese, chicken curry and beef chilli and plentiful amounts of fruit and vegetables – not a mundane menu. It also demonstrates that you don't have to be vegetarian to save the planet. The diet is familiar, normal and varied. Whilst people may debate some of the detail of this report, we firmly believe the overall story won't change. It's about small steps, doing what you can. Eat more plants, don't make meat the central component of a meal, don't replace meat with dairy or fish. By following the *Livewell* plate you will have a healthy, sustainable diet. It contains everything we normally eat – just in different proportions.

We don't believe it is necessary to exclude meat from your diet, as it contains vital nutrients and many people love it. A diet that contains no meat, fish or animal products is perfectly healthy and tasty but it is not for

everybody. *Livewell* clearly shows that you can eat meat in moderation and be an environmentalist.

How should livestock be reared?

As regards the pros and cons of different production methods, small-scale rearing of livestock can be an efficient way to use poor quality farmland that could not otherwise grow crops. In some cases livestock is an important conservation tool in managing semi-natural habitats like plant and wildlife-rich meadows and pastures. The problem comes when we use crops like wheat and soya to feed animals on an industrial scale, as this is very inefficient.

Livewell *clearly shows that you can eat meat in moderation and be an environmentalist*

As a consumer, choose meat that has a lower footprint – locally-sourced, naturally-grazed and organic are all available – and consider reducing your meat consumption or using all the cuts from the animal. Although WWF acknowledges that some studies show increasing intensification could be a method of reducing global emissions from livestock, we understand this is a very complicated area. We are first and foremost a science-led conservation organisation; we focus on species, forests, fresh water, climate change, the marine environment and sustainable production and consumption.

In other words, we aren't experts in health and nutrition, hence the reason for working with Rowett, and we aren't experts in animal welfare, thus we are looking to organisations such as Compassion in World Farming on this. Although we're aware of the host of issues relating to our current food system, our approach is to take a holistic approach and support those that enable us to work towards our goal of One Planet Living.

Organic or not?

Organic food is good for many reasons, including in supporting local biodiversity and reducing reliance on fossil fuel-based fertilisers and pesticides – for these reasons, WWF would certainly recommend buying organic. But it isn't always an affordable solution for everyone. There are other food choices you can make that still have a powerful positive impact on the environment.

In general, we believe that agricultural systems need to be developed that are a lot less dependent on fossil fuels. Organic agriculture and utilisation of organic wastes (including human, livestock and food waste) will be needed alongside enhanced soil management, lower energy production systems and better water management.

The role of farmers

We see farmers as land mangers who provide a wide range of benefits for the environment and society. Organic farming and high nature value farming deliver a significant proportion of public goods (biodiversity, landscape, water, soil fertility and climate), and these goods are delivered through careful land management.

WWF would like to see farmers paid for these services, public pay for public goods, and as such we are campaigning for Common Agricultural Policy (CAP) reform that recognises this. We need to establish a new contract between land managers and society, recognising the vital role they play in the provision of environmental goods and services.

14 February 2011

⇨ The above information is reprinted with kind permission from Duncan Williamson, WWF UK, accessed via www.theecologist.org

WWF UK

UN urges global move to meat- and dairy-free diet

Lesser consumption of animal products is necessary to save the world from the worst impacts of climate change, UN report says.

A global shift towards a vegan diet is vital to save the world from hunger, fuel poverty and the worst impacts of climate change, a UN report said today.

As the global population surges towards a predicted 9.1 billion people by 2050, Western tastes for diets rich in meat and dairy products are unsustainable, says the report from United Nations Environment Programme's (UNEP) international panel of sustainable resource management.

It says: 'Impacts from agriculture are expected to increase substantially due to population growth increasing consumption of animal products. Unlike fossil fuels, it is difficult to look for alternatives: people have to eat. A substantial reduction of impacts would only be possible with a substantial worldwide diet change, away from animal products.'

Professor Edgar Hertwich, the lead author of the report, said: 'Animal products cause more damage than [producing] construction minerals such as sand or cement, plastics or metals. Biomass and crops for animals are as damaging as [burning] fossil fuels.'

The recommendation follows advice last year from Lord Nicholas Stern, former adviser to the Labour Government on the economics of climate change, that a vegetarian diet was better for the planet. Dr Rajendra Pachauri, chair of the UN's Intergovernmental Panel on Climate Change (IPCC), has also urged people to observe one meat-free day a week to curb carbon emissions.

The panel of experts ranked products, resources, economic activities and transport according to their environmental impacts. Agriculture was on a par with fossil fuel consumption because both rise rapidly with increased economic growth, they said.

Ernst von Weizsaecker, an environmental scientist who co-chaired the panel, said: 'Rising affluence is triggering a shift in diets towards meat and dairy products – livestock now consumes much of the world's crops and by inference a great deal of fresh water, fertilisers and pesticides.'

Both energy and agriculture need to be 'decoupled' from economic growth because environmental impacts rise roughly 80% with a doubling of income, the report found.

Achim Steiner, the UN under-secretary general and executive director of the UNEP, said: 'Decoupling growth from environmental degradation is the number one challenge facing governments in a world of rising numbers of people, rising incomes, rising consumption demands and the persistent challenge of poverty alleviation.'

As the global population surges towards a predicted 9.1 billion people by 2050, Western tastes for diets rich in meat and dairy products are unsustainable

The panel, which drew on numerous studies including the Millennium ecosystem assessment, cites the following pressures on the environment as priorities for governments around the world: climate change, habitat change, wasteful use of nitrogen and phosphorus in fertilisers, over-exploitation of fisheries, forests and other resources, invasive species, unsafe drinking water and sanitation, lead exposure, urban air pollution and occupational exposure to particulate matter.

Agriculture, particularly meat and dairy products, accounts for 70% of global freshwater consumption, 38% of the total land use and 19% of the world's greenhouse gas emissions, says the report, which has been launched to coincide with UN World Environment day on Saturday.

Last year the UN's Food and Agriculture Organization said that food production would have to increase globally by 70% by 2050 to feed the world's surging population. The panel says that efficiency gains in agriculture will be overwhelmed by the expected population growth.

Professor Hertwich, who is also the director of the industrial ecology programme at the Norwegian University of Science and Technology, said that developing countries – where much of this population growth will take place – must not follow the western world's pattern of increasing consumption: 'Developing countries should not follow our model. But it's up to us to develop the technologies in, say, renewable energy or irrigation methods.'

2 June 2010

THE GUARDIAN

Industrial fishing is destroying our planet

Factsheet from The Vegetarian Society of the United Kingdom Ltd.

The fishing industry is responsible for some of the most environmentally damaging practices affecting our seas and oceans today. Bottom-trawling (trawling for fish on the ocean floor) destroys the fragile ecosystem of the sea-bed, and while debates about quotas are reported in the news, illegal fishing remains widespread. The European Commission estimates that around 10% of seafood imports could be illegally sourced.

The very existence of many species is threatened by society's appetite for fish flesh as over-fishing has resulted in tuna, cod, swordfish and marlin populations declining by 90% during the last century. Bluefin tuna, for example, is one of the most valuable fish on the planet. There is an increasing demand for its capture, with almost one-third of its catch from the Mediterranean alone arising from illegal and unregulated fishing. In September 2009, the European Commission gave its backing for a suspension of international trade in endangered Atlantic and Mediterranean bluefin tuna – expressing grave concern regarding the status of the species, which is under threat of collapse from commercial over-exploitation. Britain also indicated its support for an international ban on the sale of bluefin tuna which is threatened by over-fishing. Bluefin tuna are considered a highly valued delicacy in many parts of the world where a fully grown tuna can command up to £60,800 at market. The European Commission tabled a proposal for this species to be listed at a meeting of Convention on International Trade in Endangered Species (CITES) which took part in March of this year: the proposal was defeated. According to the European Union Commission, bluefin tuna stocks alone have fallen by 85% since the 1950s.

In a report released in October 2006 by the International Council for the Exploration of the Sea (ICES), they stated that the overall state of fish stocks has not improved much from 2005 to 2006. ICES are an organisation that coordinates and promotes more research in the North Atlantic. The report advised that numerous stocks are too heavily fished and that some stocks are depleted, e.g. cod and sand eel in the North Sea.

The 2008 World Review of Fisheries and Aquaculture stated that 19% of major commercial marine fish stocks monitored by the FAO are overexploited, 8% are depleted and 1% are ranked as recovering from depletion. The existence of many species is threatened by society's appetite for fish flesh. A major study in 2006 predicted that all commercial fisheries could die out by 2050. This four-year analysis was the first to examine all existing data on ocean species and ecosystems in order to understand the importance of biodiversity at the global scale. Results revealed that the global trend is a serious concern and projects the collapse (90% depletion) of all species of wild seafood that are currently being fished by the year 2050.

Ministers for the European Union reached an agreement for 2009 fishing quotas. In the UK, fishermen secured greater quotas of some types of fish with increased catch limits, including: 30% more North Sea cod, 32% more mackerel, 13% more North Sea plaice and 8% more monkfish for the West of Scotland, along with a reduction in the prawn quotas. The number of fish caught is likely to decline further for several decades to come, not because we are eating less fish but because they simply aren't there to be caught.

Over-fishing has resulted in tuna, cod, swordfish and marlin populations declining by 90% during the last century

Fish farming is responsible for pollution and endangering wildlife. Farmed fish have to eat, and the feeding of carnivorous fish intensifies the pressure on the oceanic fisheries. For example, it takes five tonnes of wild caught fish to feed each tonne of farmed salmon. Other concerns include the prospect of farmed salmon escaping into the wild and breeding, thus weakening the wild salmon's capacity to survive. There is also the issue of the large quantities of waste which fish-farming creates. In Scotland alone, for example, it has been reported that over three years alone salmon farmers have breached pollution limits more than 400 times.

Researchers are constantly trying to develop genetic engineering techniques in the hope of producing fish with greater economical value. The addition of an extra set of chromosomes (triploidy) is often used to produce sterile all-female fish which will not interbreed with wild populations if they escape. This genetic modification affects both the health and welfare of the fish with higher levels of spinal deformities being found in triploid rainbow trout. Scientific advisors to the UK Government say that the implications of genetic modification in fish farming are 'too risky' in that fish should not be farmed in pens set in rivers or the sea. There is the possibility that fish might escape into the environment with unforeseeable consequences.

Destructive fishing practices have spread in some poor coastal communities; for example, the use of dynamite and poison. In the Philippines, explosives are used on coral reefs to capture fish. The shock waves can kill fish in a radius of 50m from the site of blast. The use of dredges also causes changes in the bottom structure and microhabitats. Dredging is used for harvesting oysters, clams and scallops from the seabed.

⇨ The above information is reprinted with kind permission from The Vegetarian Society of the United Kingdom Ltd. Visit www.vegsoc.org and www.youngveggie.org for more information.

Becoming vegetarian 'can harm the environment'

Adopting a vegetarian diet based around meat substitutes such as tofu can cause more damage to the environment, according to a new study.

By Nick Collins

It has often been claimed that avoiding red meat is beneficial to the environment, because it lowers emissions and less land is used to produce alternatives.

But a study by Cranfield University, commissioned by WWF, the environmental group, found a substantial number of meat substitutes – such as soy, chickpeas and lentils – were more harmful to the environment because they were imported into Britain from overseas.

The study concluded: 'A switch from beef and milk to highly refined livestock product analogues such as tofu could actually increase the quantity of arable land needed to supply the UK.'

The results showed that the amount of foreign land required to produce the substitute products – and the potential destruction of forests to make way for farmland – outweighed the negatives of rearing beef and lamb in the UK.

An increase in vegetarianism could result in the collapse of British farming, the study warned, causing meat production to move overseas where there may be less legal protection of forests and uncultivated land.

Meat substitutes were also found to be highly processed, often requiring large amounts of energy to produce. The study recognised that the environmental merits of vegetarianism depended largely on which types of foods were consumed as an alternative to meat.

Donal Murphy-Bokern, one of the authors of the study and former farming and science coordinator at the Department for Environment, Food and Rural Affairs, told a newspaper: 'For some people, tofu and other meat substitutes symbolise environmental friendliness but they are not necessarily the badge of merit people claim.

'Simply eating more bread, pasta and potatoes instead of meat is more environmentally friendly.'

Lord Stern of Bradford, the climate change economist, claimed last October that a vegetarian diet was beneficial to the planet.

The environmental merits of vegetarianism depended largely on which types of foods were consumed as an alternative to meat

He told a newspaper: 'Meat is a wasteful use of water and creates a lot of greenhouse gases. It puts enormous pressure on the world's resources. A vegetarian diet is better.'

Liz O'Neill, spokeswoman for the Vegetarian Society, told *The Times*: 'The figures used in the report are based on a number of questionable assumptions about how vegetarians balance their diet and how the food industry might respond to increased demand.

'If you're aiming to reduce your environmental impact by going vegetarian then it's obviously not a good idea to rely on highly processed products, but that doesn't undermine the fact that the livestock industry causes enormous damage.'

The National Farmers' Union said the study showed that general arguments about vegetarianism being beneficial to the environment were too simplistic.

12 February 2010

The 'Meat Free Monday' campaign

A summary of the campaign and the environmental reasons behind it.

By Amy Himsworth

What is it?

'Meat Free Monday' is a campaign launched by musician and animal welfare activist Sir Paul McCartney in June 2009. It encourages people to eat meals which are meat-free on one day a week (it doesn't necessarily have to be a Monday!).

The campaign is not the first to encourage meat eaters to occasionally forgo meat – the Belgian town of Ghent launched a large-scale effort to make every Thursday a meat-free day in May 2009.

What are the reasons behind it?

One reason promoted by the 'Meat Free Monday' campaign is the potential health benefits of following a balanced, vegetarian diet on one day each week.

'Meat Free Mondays' is a campaign launched by musician and animal welfare activist Sir Paul McCartney

However, the central issue that sparked the campaign was the environment. Many people are aware of the urgent need to reduce carbon dioxide emissions in order to slow the rate of climate change. Reducing meat consumption is one way of contributing to this reduction.

The links between meat production and climate change have been debated for several years. A UN climate scientist, Rajendra Pachauri, argued that people should consider reducing the amount of meat they eat to help combat global warming. She cited UN statistics which suggest that meat production releases more greenhouse gases into the atmosphere than transport.

People supporting the 'Meat Free Monday' objectives argue that just one meat-free day a week can make a big difference to protecting the planet. Small lifestyle changes could lead to a more sustainable future.

Sir Paul McCartney summed up the different arguments for following a 'Meat Free Monday'. He stated that it was a meaningful change which all individuals could implement easily, providing benefits ranging from better health to combating pollution and the unethical treatment of animals.

Who supports the campaign?

The campaign has a range of celebrity supporters, including actors Brad Pitt, Kate Winslet and Joanna Lumley, Chris Martin of Coldplay and comedian Russell Brand.

Sir Richard Branson, who has also backed the campaign, said that although he loved eating meat, he loved the planet even more. The Chief Executive of the Vegetarian Society, Annette Pinner, emphasised the organisation's support of 'Meat Free Monday' and any initiative that helps people to reduce their meat intake.

*You can watch Sir Paul McCartney's *Meat Free Monda*y song on YouTube: http://www.youtube.com/watch?v=NnNFryHonQo

17 June 2011

Chapter 3 VEGETARIAN NUTRITION

Vegetarian health Q&A

Answers to common questions about staying healthy on a vegetarian diet, from looking after your bones to nutrition during pregnancy.

What is a vegetarian?

A vegetarian is someone who doesn't eat meat, fish, poultry or any animal by-products such as gelatine. Vegetarians eat grains, pulses, nuts, seeds, fruit and vegetables, eggs, milk and dairy products. Vegetarians who don't eat any dairy products or eggs are called vegans.

At what age is it safe to become a vegetarian?

A vegetarian diet is suitable for all ages. However, vegetarian diets are low in vitamin D, vitamin B12 and retinols (the animal form of vitamin A).

Sources of vitamin D include margarines and fortified breakfast cereals. Sources of vitamin B12 include fortified breakfast cereals and some yeast extracts such as Marmite. Sources of vitamin A include dairy products, margarines, carrots and dark green vegetables (for example, spinach, cabbage and broccoli).

Children also need protein and iron to grow and develop. Eggs, nuts (don't give whole nuts to children under five, as they could choke), pulses (such as beans, lentils and peas) and foods made from pulses (such as tofu, houmous and soya mince) are excellent sources of protein and iron.

At what age is it safe to become a vegan?

As long as they're getting all the nutrients they need, children can be brought up healthily on a vegan diet. Children require plenty of energy to help them grow and develop. Foods that are high in energy include:

- tofu
- nut and seed butters (allergy advice should be considered before these are included in any diet)
- pulses
- fortified soya drinks and yogurts
- fortified breakfast cereals
- flaxseed and rapeseed oil (omega-3 fatty acids).

It's also important that children get enough vitamin B12 and vitamin D. Consult your GP or a dietitian to see whether vitamin drops should be included in their diet. All children aged six months to five years are advised to take vitamin D supplements to prevent deficiency.

What are the health benefits of a vegetarian diet?

If your diet is typical of many people in the UK, you'd probably benefit from eating more fruit and vegetables.

By being a vegetarian you'd also cut out saturated fat ('bad' fat) from processed meat products such as sausages, burgers and pies. Too much saturated fat can raise cholesterol, increasing the risk of heart disease and stroke.

A vegetarian is someone who doesn't eat meat, fish, poultry or any animal by-products such as gelatine

Are vegetarians healthier than non-vegetarians?

Vegetarians are generally more health conscious and lead healthier lifestyles than non-vegetarians. Studies have suggested that, in general, vegetarians have a lower risk of heart disease, high blood pressure and diabetes.

Do vegetarians need nutrition supplements?

Vegetarians can lack vitamin B12, vitamin D, calcium, iron and zinc, which are mainly found in meat. However, by eating a balanced and varied vegetarian diet you don't need to take supplements.

NHS CHOICES

Iron and zinc are found in eggs, whole-grain cereals, pulses, green leafy vegetables and fortified breakfast cereals.

To get sufficient calcium and vitamins B2 and B12, have one serving of dairy every day. If you don't eat dairy products, try fortified soya milk, orange juice, dark leafy vegetables, sesame seeds, tahini, tofu or almonds.

As animal products provide the best source of vitamin B12 and iron, vegans who avoid animal products altogether may benefit from taking supplements. Sources of vitamin D include margarines and fortified breakfast cereals.

Vegetarians can lack vitamin B12, vitamin D, calcium, iron and zinc, which are mainly found in meat. However, by eating a balanced and varied vegetarian diet you don't need to take supplements

How can I protect my bones?

Calcium helps maintain strong bones. Good sources of calcium are dairy, leafy green vegetables, almonds, sesame seeds, dried fruit, pulses and fortified soya milks.

The body needs vitamin D to absorb calcium. Fortified margarine and spreads, cereals and egg yolks contain vitamin D. The body also makes its own vitamin D when exposed to sunshine. Bones get stronger when you use them, and the best way to do this is with regular exercise.

Am I getting enough iron?

Although meat is the best source of iron, there is iron in pulses, green vegetables (such as watercress, broccoli, spring greens and okra), bread and fortified breakfast cereals. It's easier to absorb iron from food if it's eaten with foods that contain vitamin C. Have some fruit, vegetables or a glass of fruit juice with your meal. Tea makes it harder for the body to absorb iron. Don't drink tea for 30 minutes before and after meals.

Do I need a special diet if I exercise?

You don't need a special diet for exercising if you're a vegetarian or vegan. The advice for vegetarian marathon runners, climbers, swimmers or cyclists is the same dietitians would give to non-vegetarian athletes.

Most vegetarians have enough protein in their diet for the body to grow and repair itself. If you exercise regularly eat plenty of carbohydrates (for example rice and pasta) for energy, and drink enough fluids when exercising harder.

Am I getting enough selenium?

Selenium is necessary for the immune system to function properly. Brazil nuts are a good source of selenium, so try to eat a couple on most days. Eating a small bag of mixed unsalted nuts containing Brazil nuts can be a convenient way to get your daily selenium intake.

Meat, fish and nuts are the best sources of selenium, but bread and eggs also provide some. If you eat a mostly vegetarian diet but also eat fish, you are probably getting enough selenium.

What are good vegetarian sources of omega-3?

Some vegetable oils, such as linseed, flaxseed, walnut and rapeseed, contain omega-3 fatty acids. The body is able to absorb only a limited amount of these vegetarian sources of omega-3, and evidence suggests that these fatty acids may not give you the same protection against coronary heart disease as the oils in fish.

What are good sources of protein for vegetarians?

Good sources of protein for vegetarians include nuts and seeds, pulses and beans, soya products (tofu, soya milk and textured soya protein, such as soya mince), cereals (wheat, oats and rice), eggs and reduced-fat dairy products (milk, cheese and yogurt). A variety of protein from different sources is necessary to get the right mixture of amino-acids, which are used to build and repair the body's cells.

Are Quorn products suitable for vegans?

No. Since all Quorn products contain a small amount of egg white, and most also contain milk ingredients, they are not suitable for vegans. They are a good source of protein for vegetarians.

Is it healthier to eat organic fruit and vegetables?

Vitamin and mineral levels in food vary depending on the soil the plants were grown in and when they were picked. There's no scientific evidence that organic food is healthier. Eating organic is a personal choice and many people eat organic for its environmental benefits as well as their own health. It's important to eat plenty of fruit and vegetables, whether they are organic or not.

⇨ Reproduced by kind permission of the Department of Health. Visit www.nhs.co.uk for more information.

NHS CHOICES

Can some nutrients be missing from, or at low levels in, the vegetarian diet?

Information from Nestlé.

The nutrient needs of vegetarians are exactly the same as those eating meat and fish. It does not matter what style of eating is followed, if a wide range of foods are not eaten as part of a healthy diet then some nutrients can fall below the level of intake that is needed for good health. Below is some information about nutrients which could be a problem in a vegetarian diet.

Protein

Protein is found in a wide range of foods, including meat, fish and dairy products. However, vegetarians get their protein from a wide range of other foods, including:

- nuts and seeds
- beans and pulses such as soya, baked beans, lentils and chick peas
- eggs
- plant sources such as cereals (wheat, maize and rice), and
- mycoproteins, commonly known as Quorn.

Animal foods such as meat, fish and eggs tend to have all of the essential amino acids, while plant foods tend to be low in one or more of these. For this reason the concept of combining proteins is important for vegetarians to ensure that they are getting all the amino acids that they need every day. It sounds complicated, but in fact is quite simple as we naturally tend to combine different sources of protein anyway, for example:

- baked beans and toast
- breakfast cereals and milk
- rice with lentil or chickpea dhal
- houmous and pitta bread.

Iron

Iron is a mineral important for healthy growth and development in children and for healthy blood in adults. Meat is the best source of iron as the body is able to absorb the iron (haem-iron) more easily than iron from other foods. Vegetable foods that contain iron include dark green vegetables such as spinach and watercress, nuts, pulses, dried fruits and fortified breakfast cereals. These contain a type of iron called non-haem iron.

When eating plant sources of iron (non-haem), it is important to try to combine these with a food rich in vitamin C (such as citrus fruits like oranges, lemons and limes, orange juice, lightly cooked vegetables or tomatoes) as this combination helps the body to absorb and use this type of iron. Try to eat an iron-fortified cereal every day with a glass of orange juice or a piece of fresh fruit. And then include at least one other iron-rich food every day such as a bean casserole with plenty of vitamin C-rich tomatoes, or a soya-based chilli con carne.

Calcium

Calcium is a mineral which is important for healthy bones and teeth. Intakes are less likely to be a problem in vegetarian diets that include dairy foods such as milk and cheese. However, if you don't eat these then it is important to ensure that any dairy alternatives such as soya milks are fortified with calcium. Other sources of calcium include nuts and seeds, tofu and dried fruits. However, for some people it may be necessary to take a calcium supplement. If you feel this applies to you, you may wish to discuss this with your GP or a dietitian.

Vitamin B12

A vitamin essential for healthy blood. It is only found in animal-based products so vegetarians need to take care to ensure they get enough. Milk and eggs are good sources, as are yeast extract, fortified breads and breakfast cereals (check the labels to see if this is added). Or again, it may be necessary to take a B12 supplement to ensure that intake is sufficient.

➪ The above information is reprinted with kind permission from Nestlé. Visit www.nestle.co.uk for more information.

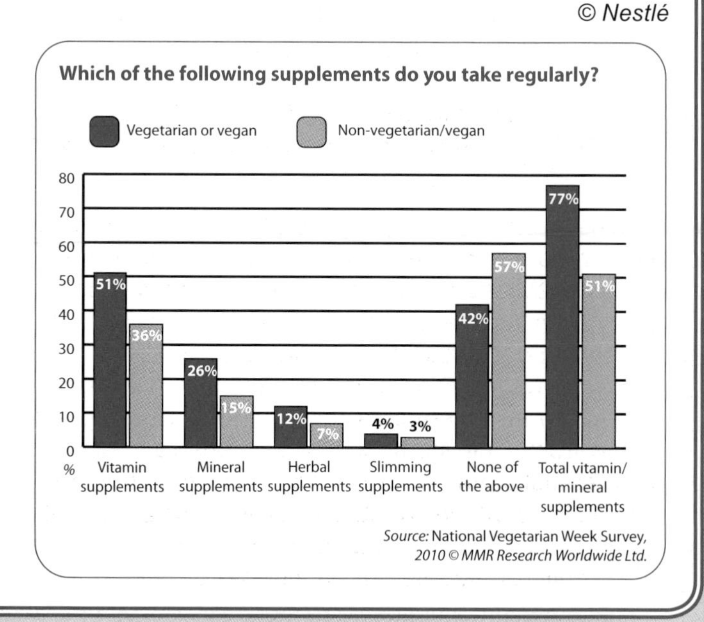

Source: National Vegetarian Week Survey, 2010 © MMR Research Worldwide Ltd.

NESTLÉ

Vegetarians 'have lower heart risk'

'Veggie diet cuts heart attack risk by a third,' according to the* Daily Express*, which reported that vegetarians are a third less likely to suffer heart problems, diabetes or stroke than meat eaters.

The results come from a small study that looked at how different dietary patterns related to the prevalence of metabolic syndrome. Metabolic syndrome is a cluster of disorders, including raised blood pressure, cholesterol and blood sugar, which increase the risk of cardiovascular disease and diabetes. The research was conducted in 773 members of the Seventh-day Adventist faith, a Christian denomination that places emphasis on staying healthy and limiting intake of meat. The researchers found that 35% of participants who considered themselves vegetarian were less likely to have metabolic syndrome or its associated risk factors than non-vegetarians.

This relatively small study is of limited value due to both its size and the fact that it assessed a very specific group of people who may not be representative of the population as a whole. Also, it only looked at people at one point in time, meaning that we cannot tell if their past behaviours influenced the prevalence of metabolic syndrome.

It has long been recognised that there may be health benefits from following a diet low in saturated fats and high in vegetables, fruit and unsaturated fats such as nut and seed oils. These health benefits include a reduction in the risk of obesity, high blood pressure and diabetes. This study does not change current healthy eating advice.

Where did the story come from?

The study was carried out by researchers from the Karolinska Institute in Sweden, Loma Linda University and the School of Public Health, Loma Linda, California. Funding was provided by the US National Institutes of Health. The study was published in the peer-reviewed medical journal *Diabetes Care*.

The news stories have, in general, not considered the numerous limitations of this cross-sectional study, including the fact that the study examined a very select population that may not reflect the behaviours or health of the general British population. Additionally, it is not clear where the 36% reduction in the risk of metabolic syndrome in vegetarians quoted in the newspapers came from. The study quoted an odds ratio of 0.44 for metabolic syndrome in vegetarians relative to non-vegetarians, which equates to vegetarian participants having a 56% lower chance of metabolic syndrome than their non-vegetarian counterparts.

What kind of research was this?

This was a cross-sectional survey of participants taking part in the *Adventist Health Study-2*, an ongoing research project studying followers of the Seventh-day Adventist religious denomination. People who follow this Christian belief system have been studied in dietary research because many adhere to special dietary habits, for example not consuming meat. Their religion also places emphasis on looking after health, particularly through avoiding habits such as smoking and drinking. Their tendency to avoid certain unhealthy lifestyle choices means that researchers can potentially discount the influence of these behaviours when performing analyses.

In this study, researchers surveyed the dietary patterns of 773 participants (average age 60 years) and assessed how their diets related to their risk of metabolic syndrome or their risk of having its individual composite risk factors (for example, cholesterol, blood pressure and high BMI). Metabolic syndrome is a cluster of disorders associated with an increased risk of diabetes and cardiovascular disease.

Studies with a cross-sectional design (which look at factors at only a single point in time) can give us proportions only, but cannot demonstrate changes or cause and effect relationships because the participants were not followed over time. Also, this particular cross-sectional study took a sub-sample of people taking part in another study, the *Adventist Health Study-2*, in which all of the participants were Seventh-day Adventists who are known to have different lifestyle and dietary habits from the general population. The selection and inclusion criteria used when enrolling people to the *Adventist Health Study-2* may mean they are not representative of the general population.

What did the research involve?

The *Adventist Health Study-2* included 96,000 people from the US and Canada, all of whom are Seventh-day Adventists, with the aim of assessing links between their lifestyle, diet and disease. At enrolment all were examined in a clinic where height, weight and blood pressure were measured and blood samples were taken to test for glucose and cholesterol levels.

Metabolic syndrome was defined according to established cut-off levels for glucose (fasting glucose

NHS CHOICES

above 100mg/dL), and they considered people to have high blood pressure or diabetes if they were taking medications appropriate to these conditions.

A food frequency questionnaire was administered and people were classed as either:

- vegetarian, if meat, poultry or fish was eaten less than once per month;
- semi-vegetarian, if any amount of fish was eaten, but meat less than once per month;
- non-vegetarian, if meat or poultry was eaten more than once per month, and in total any type of meat was eaten more than once a week.

A telephone assessment was also made to record details of alcohol consumption, smoking and exercise. The current study considered 773 of these people who had appropriate clinical and dietary information available.

What were the basic results?

The average age of participants was 60 years. Some 35% were vegetarians, 16% semi-vegetarian and 49% non-vegetarian. Body mass index (BMI) was lower among the vegetarians (25.7kg/m^2) than in the semi- (27.6kg/m^2) and non-vegetarians (29.9kg/m^2). A BMI of 18.5 to 25 is considered to be ideal weight, and a BMI of over 25 is considered to be overweight.

It has long been recognised that there may be health benefits from following a diet low in saturated fats and high in vegetables, fruit and unsaturated fats such as nut and seed oils

Risk factors for metabolic syndrome included high levels of cholesterol or glucose, high blood pressure, a large waist circumference or a high BMI. Vegetarians were less likely to have metabolic risk factors (12% of the group had three or more risk factors), compared with semi- and non-vegetarians (in both of these groups 19% had three or more risk factors). After adjusting for other lifestyle risk factors, age and sex, the researchers found that levels of blood cholesterol, blood glucose, blood pressure, waist circumference and BMI were all significantly lower among vegetarians compared with non-vegetarians. There was also a significantly higher prevalence of metabolic syndrome among non-vegetarians than among vegetarians (39.7% vs. 25.2%). Relative to non-vegetarians, vegetarians had a 56% reduced odds of having metabolic syndrome (odds ratio OR 0.44, 95% confidence interval 0.30 to 0.64, $p<0.001$).

How did the researchers interpret the results?

The researchers conclude that 'a vegetarian dietary pattern is associated with a more favourable profile of metabolic risk factors and a lower risk of metabolic syndrome'.

Conclusion

This relatively small, cross-sectional study has found a lower prevalence of metabolic syndrome or its composite risk factors among vegetarians compared with non-vegetarians. The study report itself is brief and there are several important limitations to bear in mind:

- As this is a cross-sectional survey, cause and effect cannot be implied. Too little is known about these people, their past diets, their medical history and family history to know what may have contributed to their current state of health.
- The dietary categories were quite broad and the definitions used for vegetarian, semi-vegetarian and non-vegetarian may not be consistent with other ideas of what constitutes such a dietary pattern.
- Non-vegetarians were studied as a single group containing anybody who ate meat more than once per month. Therefore, the people in this group may have had a wide range of meat-eating behaviours, with the study making no differentiation between people who ate meat twice a month and those who might, for example, eat meat every day.
- Disease outcomes, for example, heart disease, stroke and diabetes, are not reported here. Therefore, the one-third reduction in metabolic syndrome among vegetarians does not necessarily equate to one-third lower risk of having a heart attack.
- Importantly, this was a cross-sectional assessment of a sub-sample of a very select population group taking part in a wider study examining the diet and lifestyle behaviour of Seventh-day Adventists, and how this affects their health and disease risk. The findings in this group may, therefore, not be applied more generally to the wider population.

It has long been considered that a diet low in saturated fats and high in vegetables, fruit and unsaturated fats, such as nut and seed oils, has health benefits, such as reducing risk of obesity, high blood pressure and diabetes. This study does not affect current healthy eating advice.

15 April 2011

NHS CHOICES

Meat myths

An extract from Animal Aid's* Going veggie *booklet.

I need to eat meat to get iron

Wrong! Iron is plentiful in plant foods. Baked beans, chick peas, breakfast cereals and green vegetables are all good sources and it is also found in red wine and dark chocolate! Drink a glass of orange juice with your meal as vitamin C helps your body absorb iron even more efficiently.

I must eat fish for omega-3 essential fatty acids

You do not need to eat fish to get omega-3. Other sources include plant oils, such as flaxseed, rapeseed and hemp, and these, unlike fish flesh, do not contain pollutants, such as mercury and dioxins, from the contaminated seas. Other good sources of omega-3 include nuts and seeds (especially walnuts); green leafy vegetables and grains.

I need meat to get vitamin B12

Many vegetarian foods are fortified with B12, including breakfast cereals, margarines, yeast spreads and soya products. Only a small amount (3 micrograms) is required from fortified foods per day, or 10 micrograms from a daily supplement.

I need to consume dairy products for calcium

There are many non-animal sources of calcium, including beans, dried fruit, nuts and seeds, green leafy vegetables (including broccoli, kale and parsley) and even brown bread. To ensure your bones are healthy, you need to maximise absorption and minimise calcium loss. This means limiting animal protein (including cows' milk) in your diet, as this contributes to the leaching of calcium from the body. Protein from plant sources does not leach calcium from bones and calcium from plant sources is much more readily absorbed than that from animal products.

I need to eat meat for protein

The problem with the Western diet, more often than not, is too much, rather than too little, protein. Plant-based diets provide sufficient protein from grains (e.g. rice) and pulses (e.g. beans) and these contain all the amino acids (building blocks of protein) that we need.

➪ The above information is an extract from *Going veggie* and is reprinted with kind permission from Animal Aid. Visit www.animalaid.org.uk for more information.

Vegan diet may increase risk of heart-related diseases: study

***Article from* Relax News.**

According to a study published in the *Journal of Agriculture and Food Chemistry* last month, the vegan lifestyle may increase people's risk of blood clots and the hardening of arteries – conditions which can lead to heart attacks and strokes.

The study out of Hangzhou, China, was based on a review of dozens of articles on the biochemistry of vegetarianism published over the last 30 years. While meat eaters have significantly higher cardiovascular risk factors than vegetarians, the study noted that vegans tend to have elevated blood levels of homocysteine, an amino acid related to a higher risk of coronary heart disease, and decreased levels of HDL, also known as 'good' cholesterol.

The vegan diet – which eliminates meat and all animal products, including eggs and cheese – tends to lack key nutrients like iron, zinc, vitamin B12 and omega-3 fatty acids, which can lower the risk of heart-related diseases. Omega-3 fatty acids have been shown to decrease the risk of arrhythmias, or abnormal heartbeats, slow the growth rate of plaque and lower blood pressure.

The study recommends that both vegetarians and vegans up their intake of these nutrients, either through food sources or nutritional supplements. Good sources of omega-3 fatty acids include salmon and walnuts while vitamin B12 is found in seafood, eggs and fortified milk (including soy milk).

16 February 2011

Why is red meat good for you?

It's clear from these recommendations that red meat, i.e. beef, lamb and pork, have a role to play in a healthy, balanced diet.

Meat is nutrient-rich

Red meat is naturally nutrient-rich, which means it provides a substantial amount of certain vitamins and minerals. Meat also contains water, helping it to remain lower in calories compared with other foods.

The B-vitamins thiamin and riboflavin support skin health and stimulate the release of energy from dietary carbohydrates. Niacin is also important in energy release and supports digestive health. Vitamin B6 is vital for normal immune function and helps to regulate blood sugar levels. Vitamin B12 is a building block for red blood cells and the DNA inside our cells. Phosphorus, in conjunction with calcium and vitamin D, maintains bone strength, while zinc is important for normal wound healing and muscle recovery.

Facts about fat

All of us need some fat in the diet to provide us with energy, essential fatty acids (which are not made by the body) and to help the body absorb certain vitamins. However, it is important not to have too much fat in the diet, so you should try to choose lower fat foods.

Red meat is naturally nutrient-rich, which means it provides a substantial amount of certain vitamins and minerals

Fat is made up of saturated and unsaturated fatty acids. Saturated fatty acids are usually solid at room temperature and generally come from animal sources. High levels of saturated fat in the diet can increase the amount of cholesterol in the blood and so increase the risk of heart disease.

Different food groups contribute different amounts of total and saturated fat to the diet, so it is important to choose a balanced diet which is not too high in saturated fat.

The fat content of lean red meat has reduced substantially over the past few decades. A change in farming methods and butchery techniques now means that lean beef contains as little as 5% fat, lean pork 4% fat and lean lamb 8% fat.

Unsaturated fatty acids can be good for your health. They can be divided into two groups, monounsaturated fatty acids or MUFAs, and polyunsaturated fatty acids or PUFAs. There are two families of PUFAs, the omega-3 family and the omega-6 family. Certain types of omega-3 PUFAs have been shown to be good for heart health. These omega-3 PUFAs can be found in meat produced from animals grazed on grass.

One of the best sources of omega-3 is oily fish. Health professionals inform us that our diet is lacking in omega-3, so eating meat from grass-fed beef or lamb can also contribute to a healthy level of omega-3 in your diet.

To keep the fat content of your diet low, here are some top tips:

- choose lean cuts of meat and lower-fat products;
- remove any visible fat before cooking;
- avoid frying where possible: try grilling, dry-frying, roasting or stir-frying instead;
- try not to add too much additional fat from oils, mayonnaise or dressings;
- use low-fat alternatives to other ingredients;
- remember to fill up with plenty of starchy foods, vegetables and fruit.

Protein

Proteins are an important part of every cell in our body: essential for energy, growth and repair.

Protein from food consists of extensive chains of amino acids. Non-essential amino acids can be produced in the body from other proteins or carbohydrates. However, essential amino acids cannot, and need to be consumed in the diet. Through digestion, we break down protein into free amino acids. Red meat provides an excellent source of the essential amino acids that we need (Isoleucine, Leucine, Lysine, Methionine, Phenylalanine, Threonine, Tryptophan and Valine). Following protein breakdown, free amino acids are put together in a specific order to build a new protein (protein synthesis).

Beyond protein synthesis, healthy blood lipid profiles and glucose homeostasis have been associated with higher levels of dietary protein. For long-term weight loss, improvements in satiety levels – a measure of the state of fullness between meals – has been demonstrated in those individuals who opt for protein-rich foods like red meat. Significant reductions in triglyceride, total cholesterol, LDL-cholesterol and very LDL concentrations, as well as

QUALITY MEAT SCOTLAND

healthier HDL-cholesterol, have also been associated with the consumption of lean red meat.

If we consume a diet lacking in protein, we may be compromising our body's ability to efficiently carry out protein synthesis. Protein helps to build muscle, bone, cartilage and blood. Eating sufficient quantities of protein will even improve the strength and appearance of our skin and nails. By serving as a basic structural molecule of all tissues, protein plays a fundamental role in cellular maintenance, growth and functioning of the human body.

Iron

At all stages in life we require iron, and red meat provides one of the richest sources.

Iron is essential for cell respiration and metabolism. Put simply, without it our cells would die.

Iron is vital for many processes:

- energy metabolism, DNA synthesis;
- neurological development;
- the formation of red blood cells (RBCs), growth and healing;
- normal immune functioning and reproduction.

Haemoglobin (Hb) is a protein pigment made up from Iron and found within the RBC's. The main function of Hb is oxygen uptake in the lungs, transport in the RBCs and release of the oxygen at the tissues to supply working muscles with energy. In the oxygenated state it is called oxyhaemoglobin and is bright red: this gives healthy blood its characteristic deep red appearance. In the deoxygenated state it is purplish-blue.

There are two forms of dietary iron: haem and non-haem. Iron from red meat is found in haem form and is absorbed easily by the body. Iron in plants such as lentils and beans has a different chemical structure called non-haem and is absorbed less effectively.

Deficiency

Nowadays, iron-deficient anaemia (IDA) is more common, especially amongst women, young girls and the elderly. If iron stores become low or, in extreme cases, exhausted through lack of dietary iron or blood loss, the supply of iron to the tissues can become compromised and anaemic symptoms may develop. Common symptoms include headache, lethargy, difficulty concentrating and irritability.

To aid the absorption of Iron, vitamin C is encouraged, so that is one important reason for having a balanced meal that includes vegetables and fruit.

A healthy diet including red meat should contain enough iron for most adults.

⇨ The above information is reprinted with kind permission from Quality Meat Scotland. Visit www.qmscotland.co.uk for more information.

QUALITY MEAT SCOTLAND

Is a vegetarian diet suitable for children and teenagers?

Vegetarian and vegan diets typically include a high proportion of foods rich in beneficial nutrients, such as fruits, vegetables and pulses, and, appropriately planned, can provide a highly nutritious and healthy diet.

In childhood and adolescence, a time of rapid growth and development, it is especially important to ensure the consumption of foods that provide an adequate intake of nutrients.

For infants and young children, a good supply of energy and nutrients are important to meet the high requirements of the body. Yet vegetarian and particularly vegan diets tend to be high in fibre and therefore filling, so that young children can feel full before they have taken in enough calories. Diets low in energy and fat and high in bulk may therefore pose a nutritional risk for these young age groups, and they should include nutrient-rich foods: for example, milk and cheese (for lacto-ovo-vegetarians), smooth nut* and seed butters, vegetable oils, pulses, tofu and bananas.

As milk and dairy products are currently the largest contributors of vitamins B2 and B12, calcium, iodine and phosphorus in the UK diet, should these be eliminated it is important to ensure that adequate intake of these nutrients are included in the diet. Fortified soya products and fortified breakfast cereals may be useful sources of nutrients, and vegans in particular should include a reliable source of vitamin B12 such as fortified foods or a supplement.

Children and teenagers following vegetarian diets should try to consume as wide a range of foods as possible to increase the sources of nutrients available to them. Important nutritional considerations are adequate calcium and vitamin D for bone health and iron, particularly a concern in adolescent females.

If the diets are well planned and a variety of alternative sources of nutrients are consumed, these diets can provide adequate nutrient intakes. Although restricted, these diets should try to follow the principles of the balance of good health as much as possible and replace excluded foods with suitable alternatives.

**Whole nuts should not be given to children under five years of age. If they already have a known allergy or there is a history of allergy in their immediate family, talk to your GP or health visitor before you give peanuts or food containing peanuts to your child for the first time.*

⇨ The above information is reprinted with kind permission from The Dairy Council. Visit www.milk.co.uk for more information.

My vegan diet mistakes made me ill

Rachel Smith's experience of becoming a vegan is a warning to anyone who thinks it's as simple as cutting meat and dairy products out of your diet.

Rachel, 19, a student from Leicester, was 15 when she decided to switch overnight from a mixed diet to a vegan diet.

At first she tried to eat varied and balanced meals. But after a while she stopped preparing food carefully and lost weight and lacked energy as a result.

'I didn't know a lot about the vegan diet,' she says. 'I knew I needed protein from different sources, but I wasn't good at getting a varied diet.'

It was not the first time Rachel had swapped diets. At 13 she went vegetarian, but began eating meat again after a year when she became anaemic.

After a while she stopped preparing food carefully and lost weight and lacked energy as a result

She lost a large amount of weight and felt generally weak. As concern grew for her health, Rachel was persuaded to go back to eating meat.

'As a vegetarian I was not getting a balanced diet,' says Rachel. 'I relied mostly on pre-prepared vegetarian meals, but I didn't get much variety.'

Going vegan

Two years later, she went vegan. 'I was going through a difficult time and I needed a big change in my life,' she says.

'At the beginning, I made an effort to eat well. I made all my meals from scratch but I wasn't getting much variety.'

Rachel then started going for the easy option and, instead of preparing risottos and soups as she did at first, she relied on ready meals and baked potatoes with baked beans.

'I had long school days,' she says. 'When I got home I was often so tired I didn't feel like cooking.'

She lost a lot of weight and, again, was generally lacking in energy. Her poor diet started to affect her studies and social life.

'I had trouble concentrating,' she says. 'I stopped going out with my friends because I was always too tired. I wasn't the "old Rachel" that people knew.'

She missed many school days during the last year of her GCSE exams through ill health caused by her poor diet.

The turning point came during her first year at college, where she is currently studying to become a nutritionist.

'I realised, with the help of my family, that I needed to do something about my health and I gradually started to improve my diet,' she says.

She saw an NHS dietitian, who gave her a dietary plan to help her put some of the lost weight back on.

'My health has definitely improved,' she says. 'But I still have a long way to go with putting on weight.'

Research

She has since developed a strong interest in her diet. She subscribes to vegan magazines and has built up a collection of favourite cookbooks.

'I try to go to a few vegan food festivals every year. They're great for discovering new dishes,' she says.

Her advice to others tempted to go vegan or vegetarian is to do some research on the subject before making the change.

'I don't think being a vegetarian or a vegan is any harder than having a mixed diet,' she says. 'But, as with all diets, you need to eat the right proportion and variety of foods to make sure you get essential nutrients.

'Go online. There are plenty of useful websites with vegan recipes. The Vegan Society and the Vegetarian Society are reliable sources of information.

'Check out some of the vegan festivals. If you love food you'll discover things you've never tasted before.

'Get some cookbooks and try to experiment with different foods. That's part of the fun. I don't think I've had the same meal twice in the last two months.'

⇨ Reproduced by kind permission of the Department of Health. Visit www.nhs.co.uk for more information on this and other related topics.

NHS CHOICES

Are vegetarians less prone to cancer?

We're all encouraged to eat more veg for the sake of our health, but would we be better off giving up meat altogether? Patsy Westcott reports.

We're always being told to tuck into fruit and vegetables to reduce our risk of cancer and other diseases, but few studies have examined the potential benefits of being vegetarian. Until now. A team led by Professor Timothy Key, deputy director of the Cancer Epidemiology Unit at Oxford University, recently examined the effect of a vegetarian diet on the risk of developing cancer.

The team tracked the number of cancers that developed in more than 61,000 people aged 20 to 89 over a period of 12 years. Just over 32,000 were meat eaters, over 8,000 ate fish but not meat, and almost 21,000 were totally vegetarian. The results, published in the *British Journal of Cancer*, showed that vegetarians had a 12% lower incidence of any kind of cancer. More specifically they had a 44% lower incidence of stomach cancer, a 53% lower incidence of bladder cancer and a 45% lower incidence of cancers of the blood.

It has to be said that the numbers who developed cancer were relatively small – 3,350 altogether, 2,204 of which were meat eaters, 317 fish eaters and 829 vegetarians. Just 49 people developed stomach cancer, 85 bladder cancer and 257 cancers of the blood. This makes it difficult to draw definitive conclusions. However, Professor Key observes, 'Vegetarians can be reassured that their risk of cancer may be slightly lower than their meat-eating cousins.'

Professor Key is himself a vegetarian – although for humane rather than purely health reasons. But the million-dollar question is: does eating more vegetables lower the risk of cancer or is avoiding something in meat and animal products the crucial factor?

Professor Key comments, 'The difference in the amount of vegetables consumed between the three different types of diets is fairly negligible although vegetarians do eat slightly more than meat eaters. We know from other studies that meat and processed meat increase the risk of stomach, bowel and bladder cancer. Some studies also suggest that butchers and farmers who work with animals and raw meat have a higher risk of cancers of the blood.'

This suggests that it could well be something that vegetarians don't eat rather than what they do that is the crucial factor. On the other hand a growing body of research is pointing towards a protective role for certain components found in vegetables, although much of this work has been done in the test tube and in animals, while human studies tend to be contradictory.

What does seem clear is that food components work together – for instance, compounds found in soya appear to enhance the ability of vitamin D to put the brakes on prostate cancer cells. This could explain how diets as a whole – such as a vegetarian diet – rather than single food components protect against cancer. So what are the best ways to get more veg and less meat into your diet?

Perhaps the best advice is to eat your greens – and yellows, reds and blues. Fruit and vegetables of different hues are rich in what the experts call bioactive compounds, plant chemicals that, according to research, show promise in cancer prevention.

Here's a few things you can do

- Aim for two vegetarian days a week. It's better for the environment too.
- Cut consumption of red and processed meats such as bacon, salami and sausages. The World Cancer Research Fund/American Institute of Cancer Research recommend consuming less than 500 grams a week – that's around 18oz.

SAGA

- Make sure at least 50% of your plate contains vegetables and aim for eight to 12 portions a day rather than five, which is the minimum recommended to help prevent disease.
- Brassica or cruciferous vegetables, such as broccoli, cabbage and Brussels sprouts are rich in compounds called glucosinolates that, when broken down, may interrupt cancer 'pathways'.
- Even more potent are three-day broccoli sprouts – buy seeds from health food shops and garden stores and sprout them yourself or you can buy them ready sprouted.
- Onions and garlic are rich in sulphur compounds generated by chopping or chewing. In studies these have shown promise in helping to prevent bowel, oesophageal and prostate cancer.
- Compounds called polyphenols in berries plus other nutrients may help prevent cancer development. Sprinkle them on cereals, or whiz into smoothies.
- Lignans are plant chemicals found in cashew nuts, cranberries, linseed, peanuts, raisins and rye. Studies suggest they may help reduce risk of hormone-dependent cancers, such as breast and prostate.
- Selenium found in Brazil nuts and fish looks promising against a number of different cancers, including prostate.
- Diets high in soya beans and their products such as tofu and miso are linked to lower incidence of cancer. A compound called genistein found in soya inhibits breast, prostate and bladder cancer in animals and in the test tube causes the death of lung, prostate, bladder and breast cancer cells.
- Vitamin D deficiency is linked to a higher risk of a number of cancers including colon, prostate and breast cancer. The best source is sunlight but you can also get it from fish, eggs and sun-dried shitake mushrooms.
- Tomatoes, especially when cooked, are a rich source of plant chemicals called lycopene that may help protect especially against prostate cancer.
- Cut saturated fat. Saturated animal fats are linked to a higher incidence of cancer, especially of the colon, breast and prostate.

15 February 2010

- This article is published with the kind permission from Saga. It first appeared on the Saga website at www.saga.co.uk/health

Is a vegetarian diet healthier?

The 'healthiness' of a vegetarian diet depends on how nutritionally well-balanced the diet is relative to the specific needs of the individual person.

A well-balanced vegetarian diet can provide adequate amounts of all of the nutrients required by the body in a healthy person throughout their life cycle.

Studies have suggested that following a vegetarian diet can be associated with reduced risk of certain diseases such as cancers, type 2 diabetes, cardiovascular disease, etc.

It is also important to remember that people who follow vegetarian diets are often more health-conscious in general

In addition, some studies have found that vegetarians have a lower body mass index, lower cholesterol and higher intakes of protective factors called anti-oxidants which protect the body against damage from toxins.

However, it is also important to remember that people who follow vegetarian diets are often more health-conscious in general. Therefore, it is likely that they will exercise more, drink less alcohol, avoid smoking, etc., which are all thought to contribute to reduced disease risk, and current evidence suggests that it is the combination of these factors that provides protection.

It is also important to remember that following a poorly balanced or inadequate vegetarian diet can lead to nutritional deficiencies, particularly in children and adolescents where nutrient requirements are increased.

Vegetarian diets should also be carefully monitored during pregnancy and lactation when the demand for specific nutrients increases. Nutrient deficiencies during this time can lead to health problems for both mother and child and in severe cases can lead to permanent deformities in the growing infant.

- The above information is reprinted with kind permission from The Dairy Council. Visit www.milk.co.uk for more information.

SAGA / THE DAIRY COUNCIL

KEY FACTS

- ➪ A vegan diet is perhaps the most restricting diet, and excludes all meat, poultry, fish, eggs and dairy products. Vegans also avoid any food or products derived from animals, including honey, soap, leather, fur, wool or silk. (page 2)

- ➪ The key to a nutritionally sound vegan diet is variety. A healthy and varied vegan diet includes fruits, vegetables, plenty of leafy greens, whole-grain products, nuts, seeds and legumes. (page 3)

- ➪ The first usage of the term 'vegetarian' noted in the Oxford English Dictionary was as recently as 1839 – the practice and philosophy of vegetarianism, however, is far older than that. (page 4)

- ➪ Supermarkets are dropping the prominent use of the word 'vegetarian' from new meat-free dishes because they fear it puts off modern health-conscious eaters. (page 7)

- ➪ Three in five UK adults now eat meat-free food, according to consumer research for a report. However, only six per cent of adults identify themselves as vegetarians. (page 8)

- ➪ A new study of just under 6,000 UK consumers by MMR Research Worldwide reveals that the majority of vegetarians supplement their diet – 25% are 'not satisfied' with vegetarian food ranges in supermarkets, while 76% are unimpressed with fast food restaurants. (page 10)

- ➪ Meat and dairy production – now responsible for a fifth of global greenhouse gas emissions – is predicted to double by 2050. (page 16)

- ➪ Simon Fairlie, a former editor of *The Ecologist*, has challenged the received wisdom that farming meat is – or at any rate needs to be – a major cause of climate change. (page 18)

- ➪ As a consumer, choose meat that has a lower footprint – locally-sourced, naturally-grazed and organic are all available – and consider reducing your meat consumption or using all the cuts from the animal. (page 23)

- ➪ A global shift towards a vegan diet is vital to save the world from hunger, fuel poverty and the worst impacts of climate change, a UN report has said. (page 24)

- ➪ The fishing industry is responsible for some of the most environmentally damaging practices affecting our seas and oceans today. (page 25)

- ➪ A study by Cranfield University, commissioned by WWF, the environmental group, found a substantial number of meat substitutes – such as soy, chickpeas and lentils – were more harmful to the environment than meat because they were imported into Britain from overseas. (page 26)

- ➪ The Meat-Free Monday campaign is not the first to encourage meat eaters to occasionally forgo meat – the Belgian town of Ghent launched a large-scale effort to make every Thursday a meat-free day in May 2009. (page 27)

- ➪ As long as they're getting all the nutrients they need, children can be brought up healthily on a vegan diet. (page 28)

- ➪ Vegetarians can lack vitamin B12, vitamin D, calcium, iron and zinc, which are mainly found in meat. However, by eating a balanced and varied vegetarian diet you don't need to take supplements. (page 29)

- ➪ Vegetarians get their protein from a wide range of other foods, including: nuts and seeds; beans and pulses such as soya, baked beans, lentils and chick peas; eggs; plant sources such as cereals (wheat, maize and rice), and mycoproteins, commonly known as Quorn. (page 30)

- ➪ Studies have suggested that following a vegetarian diet can be associated with reduced risk of certain diseases. (page 39)

GLOSSARY

Flexitarian

Sometimes known as 'semi' or 'demi' vegetarian. A term coined to describe a diet which is mostly vegetarian but occasionally includes meat consumption, although this is often limited to only fish or white meat.

Free-range

Meat and eggs which have been sourced from animals raised in an outdoor environment with the freedom to roam around. The European Union stipulates the standards to which farmers have to adhere in order to label their produce as free-range.

Intensive farming

Intensive farming involves high levels of input (labour and cost) in order to maximise output of a product. In livestock farming, this can mean large numbers of animals cramped into a very limited space. This is sometimes called factory farming, and has been criticised for its disregard for the welfare of animals.

Meat-Free Monday

A campaign launched by Sir Paul McCartney which encourages people to have at least one meat-free day per week. The main reason behind the campaign is to reduce to the effect of meat consumption on the environment.

Meat substitute

Also referred to as meat analogues, meat substitutes imitate the texture and quality of meat but are made from non-animal products such as soya, tofu, mycoprotein or similar. Meat substitutes are popular with some vegetarians as sources of fibre and protein: others, however, dislike the taste and texture of anything resembling meat.

Omega-3

A polyunsaturated fatty acid commonly found in oily fish (such as salmon) and some nuts (such as walnuts), omega-3 is thought to reduce the risk of heart disease and aid the development of the brain.

Organic

Food which has been produced without the use of chemical fertilisers or pesticides. It takes many years for soil to become truly organic and free from any man-made chemicals. Organic food must meet certain legal standards before it can legitimately be called 'organic'.

Over-fishing

When the rate of fishing depletes fish stock to the extent that the ecological balance is upset; fish reproduction cannot keep up with the rate of depletion.

Pescetarian

A term sometimes used to describe someone who excludes all meat from their diet with the exception of fish. Some people who eat fish and no other meat choose to refer to themselves as vegetarians, however, because the term 'pescetarian' is not widely used or understood. However, eating fish means they do not follow a 100% vegetarian diet.

Protein

Proteins are chains of amino acids that allow the body to build and repair body tissue. Protein is found in dairy foods, meat and fish: it is therefore essential that a vegetarian or vegan diet includes protein from non-meat sources such as soya beans.

Quorn

Quorn is the well-known brand name of a large vegetarian food range. Quorn products are made from a type of fungi called mycoprotein.

Soya

A bushy herb native to Asia. The seed from the soybean plant is an excellent source of protein and is often used as a meat substitute.

Vegan

Someone who does not eat any animal products at all; they exclude meat, fish, poultry, dairy products, eggs and honey from their diet (any food deriving from an animal source).

Vegetarian

Someone who does not eat meat, fish, poultry or any slaughterhouse by-product such as gelatine. There are different types of vegetarian, including lacto-ovo vegetarians, who eat both eggs and dairy; ovo vegetarians, who eat eggs but not dairy; and lacto vegetarians, who eat dairy but not eggs.

ACKNOWLEDGEMENTS

The publisher is grateful for permission to reproduce the following material.

While every care has been taken to trace and acknowledge copyright, the publisher tenders its apology for any accidental infringement or where copyright has proved untraceable. The publisher would be pleased to come to a suitable arrangement in any such case with the rightful owner.

Chapter One: Going Meat Free

What is a vegetarian?, © Veggie Advisor, *Understanding different types of vegetarianism*, © Veg World, *Veganism in a nutshell*, © The Vegetarian Resource Group, *Vegetarianism: a brief history*, © Henderson's of Edinburgh, *Why vegetarian?*, © Vegetarian and Vegan Foundation, *Vegetarianism: ethics and religion*, © Vegetarian and Vegan Foundation, *Don't call it vegetarian, it is 'meat free'*, © Telegraph Media Group Limited 2011, *Meat-free foods*, © Mintel, *The health benefits of eating Quorn products*, © Marlow Foods, *Vegetarians are 'not happy' with food, says new research*, © MMR Research Worldwide Ltd, *Appearance matters more than taste for meat substitutes*, © Next Generation Food, *Being veggie: frequently asked questions*, © The Vegetarian Society of the United Kingdom Ltd., *Why I stopped being a vegetarian*, © Guardian News and Media Limited 2011.

Chapter Two: Vegetarianism and the Environment

Healthy planet eating, © Friends of the Earth, *Going veggie... for the environment*, © The Vegetarian Society of the United Kingdom Ltd., *The case for eating meat*, © MoneyWeek, *Will eating less meat save the planet?*, © Delicious, *I was wrong about veganism. Let them eat meat – but farm it properly*, © Guardian News and Media Limited 2010, *You don't have to be vegetarian to save the planet*, © WWF UK, *UN urges global move to meat- and dairy-free diet*, © Guardian News and Media Limited 2010, *Industrial fishing is destroying our planet*, © The Vegetarian Society of the United Kingdom Ltd., *Becoming vegetarian 'can harm the environment'*, © Telegraph Media Group Limited 2010, *The 'Meat Free Monday' campaign*, © Independence Educational Publishers.

Chapter Three: Vegetarian Nutrition

Vegetarian health Q&A, © Crown copyright is reproduced with the permission of Her Majesty's Stationery Office – nhs.uk, *Can some nutrients be missing from, or at low levels in, the vegetarian diet?*, © Nestlé, *Vegetarians 'have lower heart risk'*, © Crown copyright is reproduced with the permission of Her Majesty's Stationery Office – nhs.uk, *Meat myths*, © Animal Aid, *Vegan diet may increase risk of heart-related diseases: study*, © Relax News, *Why is red meat good for you?*, © Quality Meat Scotland, *Is a vegetarian diet suitable for children and teenagers?*, © The Dairy Council, *My vegan diet mistakes made me ill*, © Crown copyright is reproduced with the permission of Her Majesty's Stationery Office – nhs.uk, *Are vegetarians less prone to cancer?*, © Saga, *Is a vegetarian diet healthier?*, © The Dairy Council.

Illustrations

Pages 1, 17: Bev Aisbett; pages 2, 20, 35: Angelo Madrid; pages 3, 12, 23, 36: Simon Kneebone; pages 8, 21, 27, 38: Don Hatcher.

Cover photography

Left: © Patrycja Cieszkowska Krystosik. Centre: © Andrzej Gdula. Right: © Marijn van Braak.

Additional acknowledgements

Editorial by Carolyn Kirby on behalf of Independence.

And with thanks to the Independence team: Mary Chapman, Sandra Dennis and Jan Sunderland.

Lisa Firth
Cambridge
September, 2011

ASSIGNMENTS

The following tasks aim to help you think through the issues surrounding the vegetarian debate and provide a better understanding of the topic.

1 Definitions of what a vegetarian diet should include tend to vary: for example, some people describe themselves as vegetarian and yet eat fish. Write a short summary defining what being a vegetarian means to you. Do you think it is important to establish an accepted definition of vegetarianism, or are we free to choose our own labels?

2 Plan a three-course meal that would be suitable for a vegan diet. You should make sure each course is tasty, nutritious and balanced. You can use the Internet to help you find recipe ideas. Do you think it is difficult to plan a meal which contains no animal products at all?

3 People choose to become vegetarians for a wide range of reasons. Carry out a survey into the eating habits of the students in your class. Does everybody eat meat, fish and dairy? If not, find out what motivated that person to give up eating meat. Is there much variation in the reasons given? Display your results in a set of graphs.

4 Go into your local supermarket to research the vegetarian products they have on offer. Are they stored in a dedicated meat-free section? Is there a wide range of products available? Write a short summary of your findings, including whether or not you think the supermarket caters sufficiently for vegetarians. Compare your conclusion with the findings displayed in the graph on page 10.

5 Read *Being veggie: frequently asked questions* on page 12. Role play a segment on meat-free diets for a TV morning chat show. One student will play the host and two to three other students will play guests taking part in a discussion on vegetarian diets. You can use the question and answer structure of the Vegetarian Society article as a starting point for your script.

6 Carry out a survey of people in your year group to find out if they would eat a product labelled 'vegetarian', and if their view changes when the product is labelled 'meat-free'. What conclusions can you draw?

7 Read *Industrial fishing is destroying our planet* on page 25. Design a poster which will inform consumers about which fish products are ethical and sustainable. It should give brief information on the problems associated with over-fishing and advise on why it is important to support sustainable fishing.

8 Sir Paul McCartney launched the 'Meat-Free Monday' campaign to encourage people to give up meat for one day per week. Come up with your own campaign to persuade the British public to consider where their food comes from. It does not have to promote vegetarianism, but rather ethically-sourced food in general.

9 Design a booklet for teenagers who are considering becoming vegetarians. You should give advice on how to achieve a balanced diet without eating meat. Suggest specific foods and recipes which are good sources of protein, iron and other vital nutritional requirements which they may currently get from their meat intake.

10 Is it right that vegetarian and vegan parents bring up their children with the same meat-free eating habits? Or should children be allowed to decide for themselves what they eat? Discuss this with a partner, then write a summary of your conclusions.

11 There is an ongoing debate over whether a vegetarian diet is more or less healthy than a diet which includes meat. Carry out your own research into this issue using the articles in Chapter Three of this book as well as other sources. Write a brief summary of your findings, outlining each argument and providing your own conclusion.

12 Compare the nutritional value of a meat substitute product with an equivalent meat product, for example pork sausages with Quorn or soya sausages. Which is healthiest overall? Which contains the most protein?

13 Design the packaging for a meal in a new range of meat-free products being launched by your local supermarket. The supermarket wants the new range to have universal appeal, attracting both vegetarians and non-vegetarians who may be turned off by the idea of vegetarian food generally. How would you make the product look enticing to both these groups?